Conceptualizing society

For a century, European social anthropology has been one of the most stimulating and creative influences within the social sciences. Social theory has had to grapple with the varieties of human experience reported by ethnographers; and out of their ethnographic experience, social anthropologists have constructed unique theoretical insights. The contributors to this volume, leading figures in European social anthropology today, reanimate this great tradition. They confront the models current in the social sciences with the diverse, often exotic, experiences and models of their subjects.

But if the broad project is accepted, theoretical strategies are the subject of urgent debate. The authors in this volume advocate diverse approaches to social theory, ranging from the action-based models of network theorists through the subtleties of the neo-structuralists to the daring experiments of the new cognitivists. Their lively debates refer to fascinating case studies, drawn from wide ethnographic experience.

Conceptualizing Society represents a significant contribution to social theory. It will be required reading for all social anthropologists, and for all those whose concern with social theory transcends the most parochial span.

EUROPEAN ASSOCIATION OF SOCIAL ANTHROPOLOGISTS

The European Association of Social Anthropologists (EASA) was inaugurated in January 1989, in response to a widely felt need for a professional association which would represent social anthropologists in Europe, and foster co-operation and interchange in teaching and research. As Europe transforms itself in the 1990s, the EASA is dedicated to the renewal of the distinctive European tradition in social anthropology.

Other titles in the series

Revitalizing European Rituals
Jeremy Boissevain

Other Histories
Kirsten Hastrup

Alcohol, Gender and Culture
Dimitra Gefou-Madianou

Understanding Rituals
Daniel de Coppet

Conceptualizing society

Edited by
Adam Kuper

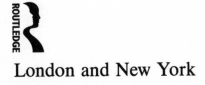

London and New York

First published in 1992
by Routledge
11 New Fetter Lane, London EC4P 4EE

Simultaneously published in the USA and Canada
by Routledge
a division of Routledge, Chapman and Hall, Inc.
29 West 35th Street, New York, NY 10001

Typeset in 10/12pt Times by
Falcon Typographic Art Ltd, Fife, Scotland
Printed and bound in Great Britain by
Biddles Ltd, Guildford and King's Lynn

British Library Cataloguing in Publication Data
A catalogue record for this book is
available from the British Library.

Library of Congress Cataloging in Publication Data
Conceptualizing society / edited by Adam Kuper.
  p. cm.
  The first of six volumes of papers from the first
  conference of the European Association of Social
  Anthropologists held in the summer of 1990 in Coimbra,
  Portugal.
  Includes bibliographical references and index.
  1. Ethnology – Philosophy – Congresses. I. Kuper,
  Adam.
  II. European Association of Social Anthropologists.
  GN345.C655   1992
  305.8'001 – dc20   91–43623
                                              CIP

ISBN 0–415–06124–5
    0–415–06125–3 (pbk)

Contents

Part III Models of society, the individual, and nature

Contributors

Fredrik Barth is Research Scholar at the University of Oslo and Professor of Anthropology at Emory University. His extensive fieldwork has taken him to the Northwest Frontier in Pakistan, Iran, Darfur in the Sudan, Papua New Guinea, Oman, Bali, and Bhutan. He has published a number of influential monographs, the most recent being *Cosmologies in the Making: A Generative Approach to Cultural Variation in Inner New Guinea* (Cambridge: Cambridge University Press, 1987).

Maurice Bloch is Professor of Social Anthropology at the London School of Economics and Political Science. He has done extensive fieldwork in Madagascar, and his most recent monograph is *From Blessing to Violence: History and Ideology in the Circumcision Ritual of the Merina of Madagascar* (Cambridge: Cambridge University Press, 1986).

Daniel de Coppet is Directeur d'Etudes, Ecole des Hautes Etudes en Sciences Sociales, Paris. He has engaged in long-term fieldwork in the Solomon Islands, making six expeditions since his first in 1963, and he has also done fieldwork in the Moluccas. His publications include many articles and (with H. Zemp), *'Are 'Are: Un peuple Mélanésien et sa musique* (Paris: Editions du Seuil, 1978).

Philippe Descola is Directeur d'Etudes, Ecole des Hautes Etudes en Sciences Sociales, Paris, and co-director of the Laboratory of Social Anthropology at the Collège de France. He has done a total of more than three years' field research in Amazonia and is the author of books and articles including *La nature domestique* (Paris: Editions de la Maison des Sciences de l'Homme, 1986).

Ulf Hannerz is Professor of Social Anthropology at Stockholm University. He has done field research in Washington, D.C., the Cayman Islands, and Nigeria and published both ethnographic and theoretical studies, among which is *Cultural Complexity* (New York: Columbia University Press, 1992).

Adam Kuper is Professor of Social Anthropology at Brunel University. He has done fieldwork in the Kalahari desert and in Jamaica, and his most recent monograph is *The Invention of Primitive Society: Transformations of an Illusion* (London: Routledge and Kegan Paul, 1988).

Marilyn Strathern is Professor of Social Anthropology at Manchester University. She has done long-term fieldwork in Papua New Guinea and published a number of books and articles, most recently *The Gender of the Gift: Problems with Women and Problems with Society in Melanesia* (Cambridge: Cambridge University Press, 1988).

Preface

The first conference of the newly formed European Association of Social Anthropologists (EASA), which was held in Coimbra, Portugal, in the summer of 1990, brought together social anthropologists from all over the continent. The various panels reflected diverse contemporary concerns, but there was a vivid sense that social anthropology retains a distinctive identity and is set to renew itself. It is still very largely a European tradition within the social sciences, but European self-consciousness is in a process of transformation, and social anthropology today is an open tradition influenced by developments in European sociology, historiography, and philosophy, by American cultural anthropology, and by cognitive science. Six collections of papers from the conference are being published to launch a new series of EASA papers in social anthropology. This volume, the first, is the record of one of the panels which inaugurated the Coimbra meetings.

Adam Kuper
London, March 1991

Introduction

Adam Kuper

The title of this volume is deliberately ambiguous, since the problem facing the social anthropologist is to reconcile at some level the experiences and conceptualizations of actor and observer. Sociologists may assume that they know what the natives think: social anthropologists know that their first task is to find this out, their next to make sense of a foreign experience without sacrificing its particularity.

Make sense for whom? Social anthropologists typically take their bearings within the social science community (or, as many now prefer to see it, the field of the human sciences). However, they refuse to serve it merely as middlemen, importing exotic data for the delectation – or discomfiture – of theorists. Indeed, they are likely to reject on principle the characteristic division of labour in the social sciences between the theorist, or synthesizer, and the experimentalist, or fieldworker. The complete modern social anthropologist aspires to be both an ethnographer, in the manner of Malinowski, and a model-builder or theorist.

Each aspect of this double role deserves sceptical scrutiny, but attention has recently focused particularly on the role of the ethnographer – a role which American 'post-modernists' have taken apart with such ferocity that some young ethnographers seem almost to despair of its possibilities. ('They are . . . harassed by grave inner uncertainties,' writes Clifford Geertz, 'amounting almost to a sort of epistemological hypochondria, concerning how one can know that anything one says about other forms of life is as a matter of fact so' [Geertz 1988: 71].)

Where the theorists of post-modernism would render ethnography impossibly problematic, some prominent social anthropologists have taken a contrary point of view. In certain moods, revolting against modish theories, Evans-Pritchard and Schapera, for example, would describe themselves as 'ethnographers' rather than as 'social anthropologists', their argument being that ethnography had eternal validity but no theory could do justice to its insights and complex descriptions. They have their counterparts today, perhaps burnt by theoretical misadventures, who would also be content with a particularist, descriptive enterprise.

Others would argue that, while ethnography cannot pretend to produce objective 'truth', it remains the only plausible theoretical project. The ethnographer interprets and so, in a sense, explains, while recognizing that each interpretation is partial and provisional, being limited by the perspective of the ethnographer and the cultural experience of the audience being addressed. On this view, the human sciences are themselves culturally specific productions, their theories of interest only if one is studying Western intellectuals. The one theory which escapes this relativizing process is, of course, the relativist theory which puts out of bounds all other theories (including the point of view which would marginalize it as 'relativist').

The social anthropologists represented in this volume accept the more conventional view that ethnographic research yields findings which can be reinterpreted in different analytical frameworks and compared with similar data collected elsewhere, by other ethnographers. Cross-cultural theoretical argument is by no means a doomed, sterile exercise in projection. Together, ethnography and theoretically informed comparison constitute a single plausible enterprise.

This brings us back to the most curious and also the most characteristic fact about the social anthropologist's programme: it is still expected to combine ethnography with theory (or model-building or comparison), although today ethnography is generally regarded as the privileged partner. The social anthropologist's aim is to contribute to the human sciences not only indirectly, by adding to the ethnographic record, but directly and yet *as an ethnographer*.

Every professional social anthropologist is expected to have had first-hand ethnographic experience. This exposure to another culture is the *rite de passage* for entry to the profession. It is also assumed to provide a necessary basis for making theoretical contributions to the discipline. The evocation of personal ethnographic experience is a routine – almost ritualized – preliminary to theoretical discourse. The orthodoxy, usually implicit but perhaps all the more powerful for that, is that ethnography constitutes the rock on which is founded the special contribution of social anthropology to the human sciences.

The typical refusal of social anthropologists to countenance a separation between fieldworker and theorist is doubly curious in that it is a relatively modern development. The founding fathers assumed that there *should* be a division of labour between the theorist (metropolitan, detached, study-bound) and the fieldworker (colonial, dedicated to a particular people, bushwhacking). Frazer was famously horrified at the suggestion that he might undertake his own field research, and Marett assumed that there was necessarily a hierarchical ordering of the two prototypical figures whom he termed 'the man in the study' and 'the man in the field' (Marett 1927: 4). Although Haddon – a hardy fieldworker himself, and writing after Malinowski had published his major Trobriand monographs – remarked that 'the most valuable generalizations are made . . . when the observer is at the same time a generaliser', he immediately followed up by quoting Maharbal's remark to Hannibal after the battle of Cannae: 'The gods have not bestowed everything on the same man. You, Hannibal, know how to conquer; but you do not know how to use your victory' (Haddon 1934: vi). Even Boas, Rivers, and Radcliffe-Brown respected this division of labour in principle. They were all in practice both theorists and ethnographers, but they insisted that their observations be kept separate from their theories. Description and analysis were distinct operations, susceptible to mutual contamination.

The breaching of this boundary between fieldwork and theory was accomplished only as a consequence of Malinowski's fieldwork revolution. Malinowski had studied Mach, and he expressed radical ideas about the way in which 'facts' were constructed by theories. He was also ready to deploy his own field observations in theoretical debates, moving directly from Trobriand ethnography to questions of grand theory. Malinowski would put some general thesis about human nature, or about 'savages' to the test of his own observations on a remote Pacific island and refute it. Alternatively, he would suggest that Trobriand behaviour exemplified some general principle of sociology or psychology. People everywhere were – like the Trobriand Islanders of his descriptions – practical, utilitarian, manipulative, and their institutions suited their very rational purposes. Social institutions hung together because together they performed necessary tasks. Malinowski, then, is the classic exemplar of the modern social anthropologist, the fieldworker as theorist. This heroic task was legitimated by the argument that the fieldworker, uniquely placed to appreciate the function of institutions in action, was in a privileged position to develop a theoretical understanding of a society.

In the second half of the century, functionalism fell out of favour, and many anthropologists became more interested in problems of meaning and interpretation. This move, however, gave fresh impetus to the integration of the roles of fieldworker and theorist. For Malinowski, it was only the fieldworker who could appreciate how things hung together and what motivated actors. Those influenced by the phenomenological theories which became popular in the post-war period came to believe that only the ethnographer – and then only the most skilled and sensitive ethnographer – could really understand what mattered most, which was the actor's construction of reality, his conceptualization of society.

The shift of emphasis from the observer's model to the actor's model precipitated a radical shift in the balance of power between ethnographer and theorist (even if these two roles were now ideally combined in one person). If the actor constructs a world of meaning within which actions are generated and interpreted, then it can be argued that a fresh theory must be minted for every culture – or, perhaps, that the ethnographer, at once witness and interpreter, must reconstruct the particular theory of the actors under study. At the same time, sociological generalizations become suspect. They are likely to represent no more than a folk model of the West masquerading as a universal scientific theory, although quite unsuited to the interpretation of foreign ways of life. The ethnographer should not be fooled. His task is to confront this culturally specific Western vision with a counter-theory which bears witness to the experience of his subjects. Life is not like that, he tells the theorist; you are working on the preposterous assumption that everyone in the world behaves like late-twentieth-century citizens of industrial democracies. And so the ethnographers, grubby hands, sweaty work clothes, and all, are not content to demand a place at the theorists' table: they intend to drive the theorists from their meal.

DURKHEIM AND MALINOWSKI

The theorists confronted by modern social anthropologists are still commonly the classical figures in Western sociology – notably Durkheim and Mauss, but also at times Marx, or Weber and Simmel. Within this broad tradition, however, two divergent formulations have stubbornly confronted each other. These might crudely and provisionally be termed Malinowskian and Durkheimian. The modern Malinowskian is concerned with individual agents. Structures are simply the record deposited by their strategies, and values are the conventions they invoke when they try to influence the behaviour of others. A Durkheimian, in contrast, believes that collective representations and agencies inform the actions of the socially constituted individual – although for Durkheim and Mauss this was true above all of 'traditional' societies, modernity being marked by the decay of communal identities and the rise of individualism.

Malinowski himself started as a Durkheimian, but he later adopted an individualistic sociology of strategies and goals that was more compatible with the methodological directions of Simmel and indeed of Weber (although Weber notoriously did not apply them in his own substantive work). Radcliffe-Brown and Mauss developed the Durkheimian tradition, if in rather different directions; for Mauss the social reality was to be found in collective representations, while for Radcliffe-Brown the structure of social relations was primary and determined the collective representations. Even Lévi-Strauss claimed to be, if not exactly a Durkheimian, then still a Maussian. His *Elementary Structures of Kinship* can be read as a Maussian rejoinder to the individualist, economistic theory of cross-cousin marriage which Frazer had advanced and which Malinowski, naturally, favoured.

The classical sociological writers were trying to express the difference between traditional and modern society. Contemporary social anthropologists are confronted with post-colonial societies and, some would say, a post-modern world. New frameworks have been developed to give an account of this new world, and social anthropologists have tapped them. In the 1970s Marxism was seen by some as a promising way of reintegrating ethnographic work with models of broader social change. World-systems theory still has its adherents among anthropologists, and Hannerz's essay in this volume addresses some of its concerns. More recently, the deconstructionist critique of modernist theories has made converts, and Strathern integrates some 'post-modernist' themes into her argument here. Cognitive science is also being taken seriously by some anthropologists, as may be seen from Bloch's contribution.

Unfortunately, despite this eclecticism, more mainstream but innovative sociological theorists have been neglected. Among them are writers who have attempted to transcend the opposition which dogs social anthropology between theories stressing individual agency and more structural approaches. The names of Bourdieu, Giddens, and Archer are notable absentees from bibliographies in this volume (see, e.g., Archer 1988; Bourdieu 1972; 1980; Giddens 1984; 1990; cf. Bryant and Jary 1991). Despite the shifts in fashion of the past twenty years, social anthropologists can still often be classed – roughly, and probably much against their will, but not altogether unfairly – as Durkheimians or Malinowskians. Among the contributors to this volume, Barth and Hannerz draw upon a recognizably Malinowskian perspective in defining modern social experience (though Hannerz invokes Radcliffe-Brown's notion of social networks), while de Coppet, for instance, renews the tradition of Durkheim, Mauss, and even Tönnies.

ACTS, INDIVIDUALS, AND NETWORKS

Ulf Hannerz suggests that the traditional Durkheimian vision – one society, one culture for each person – might have been appropriate to 'the prototypical small-scale society, in which people exposed to much the same living conditions have similar personal experiences and are at the same time available to a massively redundant communication flow only from people largely like themselves'. It is the modern world itself which has rendered the traditional model obsolete. There are no bounded societies any longer. Few people can still enjoy the comfort of a single, unified and coherent view of life. Rather, 'different meanings and meaningful forms may occur in different social relationships, and . . . the cultural contents of more or less adjacent relationships may impinge on one another'. The ethnographer, even if recording social life in the most apparently isolated corner of the world, faces 'the task of illuminating the influence of wider structures, usually of alien origin, on local life'. Everybody's experience is ultimately touched by global social processes.

Fredrik Barth argues that the Durkheimian model was always an illusion, the product of a European fantasy that humanity is divided into units approximating bounded nation-states, each with its jealously guarded frontier, language, and culture. The truth is rather that 'societies' are always and everywhere open and disordered. There is no expectation of 'repetition, norms, and shared ideas as blueprints for acts and prerequisites for social action'. Biculturalism, scepticism about conventional values, continual adaptation to fresh situations – these are the norms. This is evident when we consider the social experience of even the most isolated human populations.

The ethnographic exemplar which Barth has chosen is the situation of villagers in pre-war Afghanistan. They were involved in a complex of economic activities in an environment which embraced farmers, pastoral nomads, absentee landowners, and state bureaucrats. Religious and political affiliations brought them into relationships with citizens of a large market town and with clerics in various small religious centres. There were 'startling discrepancies in scale between the ways activities in different fields in this particular social formation were organized and the processes whereby groups were constituted'. Grönhaug, the ethnographer on whose work he draws, 'found no basis on which any one of these fields or any one organizational scale and territorial span could be selected to define an encompassing "society"'.

Since we cannot sensibly take an imaginary 'society' as our unit of analysis, Barth urges us to begin with the elementary constituent of social action, which he takes to be the social event. This is a meaningful 'act' if it is imbued with purpose or interpreted (perhaps mistakenly) as being purposeful by an onlooker. Social interactions are sequences of acts and responses. Each act entails an attempt to interpret and predict responses, and in consequence 'there will tend to be a certain convergence of interpretations between the parties to such sequences even where their interests remain distinct and their strategies opposed'.

For Barth, a broader context is constituted by 'overlapping social networks with crosscutting boundaries'. This comes close to Hannerz's view: he too prefers the image of social networks to that of a 'society'. The actor participates in a series of divergent networks, guided not by culturally set values but by 'flows of meaning' through various networks of relationships. His ethnographic type-cases of this global experience are not supposedly exemplary villages in Afghanistan, New Guinea, or India but three individual

European converts to Islam, neither-Western-nor-Eastern citizens
of the present.

VALUES, ACTS, AND VALUE-FACTS

For de Coppet, individualist sociologies of the sort favoured by
Barth and Hannerz are projections not of the post-modern experience but of a modern ideology – indeed, the characteristic ideology
of the modern world – in which the individual is the primary source
of value and 'society' a vaguely conceived external constraint,
morally suspect if not wholly imaginary (as Mrs Thatcher, that
prophet of individualism, roundly proclaimed). Following Louis
Dumont, de Coppet identifies a system of values as the structuring
principle of social life; but these values are not, as in individualist
sociologies, to be distinguished from acts. The neo-Malinowskian,
for instance, tends to treat each person's acts as though they were
motivated by straightforward calculations of individual advantage,
even if, as in Barth's formulation, rational expectations rest on
the shaky basis of partial information. De Coppet insists, on the
contrary, that acts express values, values imbue acts. Moreover,
the values characteristic of a particular system form an ordered,
hierarchical structure. The characteristic modern weighting of the
'individual'/'social' contrast (in which the individual threatens to
swallow up the social) inverts an alternative ordering characteristic
of traditional societies in which the individual is represented as a
subordinate part of a larger, more valued whole.

It is such total systems of value which Dumont instructs us
to compare, arguing that only whole systems of this sort are
truly comparable, and then only if we transcend the ideological
bias of Western individualism. Dumont achieves the necessary
distance from our contemporary ideology by placing it in contrast
to India, his particular 'other', and by reconstructing its historical
transformations (see Dumont 1977; 1986). In a similar vein, de
Coppet treats two dominant Western notions of 'representation',
contrasting the idea of representation as symbol or substitution,
which has been adopted by those sociologies which would divide
a presumed social reality from its ideological images, and the more
ancient notion of representation as re-enactment. Collective representations, de Coppet insists, are re-enacted in this latter sense.
They are not external, constraining communal values which can be
separated analytically from the expression of rational, individual

interests. The characteristic unit of social life is neither individual act nor social value but the re-enactment of values; and these form systems which may be compared.

WHOLE PERSONS

De Coppet suggests that a holistic sociology does more justice to the conceptualizations of society characteristic of traditional communities, and he has attempted to illustrate this proposition in his own Melanesian ethnographic writing. Marilyn Strathern, who engages his approach most directly, is herself a Melanesianist, and she bases her critique on a very different reading of the way in which Melanesians constitute the social world. She agrees that 'the society we think up for the 'Are 'Are, Melanesians from the Solomon Islands [to whom de Coppet has devoted much of his career as an ethnographer], is a transformation of the society we think up for ourselves', but against de Coppet she insists that if we analyse such a Melanesian society in its own terms we will recognize that the people offer not a holistic vision but a conceptualization of various partial, incomplete, fragmented relationships. The central notion in her account is neither 'society' nor the naked individual but the social actor, the 'person', and persons are described not as wholes but as the temporary sum of independent parts which may be – indeed, regularly are – taken to pieces again. Her case is that contemporary Melanesian ethnography 'describes the processes by which the elements that compose persons are dismantled so that the relationships persons carry can be invested anew'.

As does de Coppet, Strathern argues that Melanesian conceptions of social relations do not match those which classical sociology imposes on Melanesian ethnography: but she has in mind very different sociological models from those which he criticizes. The established models of sociology are not, in her argument, the individualist constructs of the Malinowskians but rather those developed by the holistic sociologies which have pervaded social anthropology since Durkheim and have been most recently developed by such writers as Dumont. She regards these holistic models as being themselves in tune with our own folk sociology, which is not simply individualistic but presupposes a 'society' that gives the individual an identity and purpose. In our folk sociology, a child has to be 'socialized', completed by society. Death cuts off persons from the relationships which they have established in their lifetimes.

The characteristic Melanesian idea is that the individual person embodies a world of social relations, but a world which can be – and regularly is – picked apart and reconstructed. Massim mortuary ceremonies 'strip the deceased of social ties: the enduring entity is depersonalized'.

According to Strathern, Melanesians do not imagine that their experience can be organized by an overarching framework – 'society' – embracing all the persons with whom they interact. The persons of Melanesian social theory embody individual and shifting configurations of social relationships, but they are not members of a greater unity. For precisely this reason, Melanesian notions may point the way to a more realistic social theory for the post-modern world than that offered by our traditional folk sociology, at least to the extent that it imposes a holistic vision upon social relations. There is even a convergence between Melanesian perspectives and those of the post-modernists in anthropology, who aim to capture the experience of Hannerz's new citizen of nowhere and to deconstruct the holistic illusions of modernist theory.

Nevertheless, Strathern stops short of electing the Melanesians as our preferred guides to the contemporary world, warning that 'one should be as cautious as one is creative with the resonances between cultural fragmentation perceived in the world at large, specific analytical tactics such as deconstruction, and the discovery of relationship being indigenously conceptualized through images of dissolution'. Equally, she notes that Hannerz's view of a hybrid, global, post-plural social field may itself represent a particular modern Western perspective, and one which cannot be generalized.

THE STRUCTURE OF KNOWLEDGE

Maurice Bloch and Philippe Descola are less ready to specify actors' models in propositional form as though they constituted full-blown alternatives to our own social theories. Indigenous theories of social experience are not coherent, explicit constructs conveniently packaged for the ethnographer's appraisal. Descola points out that most people 'do not spontaneously picture their cultures as systematic wholes. Rather, they haphazardly combine partial points of view and elicited intuitions, scraps of knowledge and appeals to tradition, to produce – unknowingly and collectively – something approximating to the global image mirrored by the monograph'. Moreover, the ethnographer's models are not easily retranslated into terms which make sense to their subjects. Bloch remarks that 'the way anthropologists conceptualize the societies they have studied in their ethnographic accounts almost always seems alien, bizarre, or impossibly complicated to the people of those societies. Perhaps this would not matter if ethnographies claimed only to be description from the outside; however, most accounts attempt, at least in part, to represent a society and ways of thinking about it from the insiders' point of view'.

Bloch and Descola draw similar conclusions from this mismatch between the models of observer and actor. The social anthropologist should penetrate beyond the partial models of the actors and develop a theory about the modes of thought which constitute these exotic worlds. They argue that folk models exhibit forms of reasoning which are becoming increasingly familiar in cognitive science. Descola stresses the universal ways of classifying nature which are now being uncovered (e.g., Atran 1990), and beyond that he appeals to the workings of what Lévi-Strauss called a 'science of the concrete'. Bloch gives a vivid and plausible account of Zafimaniry thinking in terms of connectionist theory, also bringing out the concreteness of their cognition and the place within it of natural referents. The idea is that folk sociologies may be decoded if their underlying principles of construction are appreciated. They may then also turn out to have a great deal in common at the level of content – perhaps, as both Descola and Bloch suggest, because they build upon cognitive universals and, in particular, upon universal ways of thinking about nature.

A central theme for both is the way in which folk models integrate conceptions of social relations and conceptions of nature. They describe folk models which bring together human beings and natural objects within a single conceptual space. Bloch shows how the Zafimaniry think about social maturation in terms of processes which affect people, trees, wooden posts, and houses. Inanimate objects do not function as metaphors for social processes, because social relations are not imagined to be of a different order from natural processes. Social relations are experienced as natural in part because they are learnt, picked up, together with the associated knowledge about the natural world. Descola, similarly, shows how some Amazonian peoples have created a sociology which unites human beings and animals in a single social field. The folk sociologies of many peoples are, apparently, ecologically informed. De Coppet's term for them is 'socio-cosmic systems'. They are therefore perhaps modern in another and even more relevant sense than our own conventional sociologies.

ETHNOGRAPHY, THEORY, AND COMPARISON

If these folk models can be reliably constructed and do exhibit both structural and substantive similarities, then clearly comparison and generalization are back on the agenda again. This may involve such grand interdisciplinary projects as the pursuit of cognitive universals, but social anthropologists still normally concern themselves with more limited categories of social structures and institutions.

Descola refers back to two of the classic objects of comparison which have been created by social anthropology, namely, 'animism' and 'totemism' (for a history and critique of these notions, see Kuper 1988). He introduces a third variant of nature–society thinking which he identifies among Amazonian peoples and terms 'animic systems'. As it happens, a good example is Bloch's account of the Zafimaniry identification of people, trees, and wood. Should we add the Zafimaniry to the trio of Amazonian cases which Descola describes, engaging in a cross-cultural comparison of 'animic systems'?

That is certainly one option, but there is another, closer, perhaps, to that which de Coppet might prefer. This would be to seek general principles of conceptualizing social relations not at a universal level but within a culture area of some kind. Descola effectively follows this course in his paper, which compares three historically and linguistically related sets of Amazonian cultures. Bloch's account of the construction of the Zafimaniry person might rather be related to what Strathern has to say concerning the notion of the person more generally in the Austronesian-speaking world (of which the Zafimaniry constitute a remote outpost). Her suggestion is that, in this culture area, 'the elements that compose persons are dismantled so that the relationships persons carry can be invested anew'. Bloch shows that this principle applies among the Zafimaniry, where, however, it encompasses not only persons, in our sense, but persons and what we would regard as inanimate objects, with which persons are merged. Persons and inanimate objects join in the same processes of composition and decomposition. These Austronesian models are rather different from the Amazonian models which Descola investigates, although there is certainly a level at which they seem to display similar principles of construction.

Between the individual case-study of the field ethnographer and the grand universals of the theorist there are, then, local systems of variants which exist in a particular series of landscapes and within a specific historical period. Culture areas are defined in part by historical relationships, and they may exhibit profound continuities despite superficial changes. Structural continuities within a region may signal shared roots, though local variants may be shaped by direct interactions, exchanges, even confrontations between communities, as Descola shows so elegantly for his Amazonian cases. Because of these necessary references to historical processes, regional comparison in social anthropology has an elective affinity with the historiography of the 'long term' which has been practised by some historians of the *Annales* school (and they are close associates of French social anthropology).

As Descola's paper illustrates, a regional perspective can avoid the problematic assumption, rightly criticized by Barth and Hannerz, that 'cultures' coincide with bounded 'societies'. Cultural premises may shape social relationships between communities (including even warfare), and populations completely ignorant of one another's very existence may enact structural variants of the same system of values. Within a regional context it may also be possible to transcend the opposition between structure and agency while sacrificing neither – although it must be admitted that neither Barth (for whom a region is a field of social relations) nor Descola (for whom it is culturally defined) has attempted to do so.

The essential impulse behind regional structural comparison is to reconcile comparative theoretical projects with the ethnographer's sense of what can be lost in translation. So long as the ethnographer remains the dominant partner in this enterprise, the risk is that we will remain content with broader, more elaborate ethnographies which yield general propositions but only insofar as these relate to what the Leiden scholars call an *ethnologisch studieveld*. Ultimately this may amount to no more than a shift in the range of our ethnographic investigations. Unless regional comparisons are informed by more comparative or generalizing projects, they will have little to contribute to the social sciences, however much they may enrich the understanding of particular cultural traditions or political processes.

This introduction is an attempt to explain that the apparently very diverse papers collected in this volume have a common premise. They realize, in different ways, the dual function of the social anthropologist – build upon the two roles which the social anthropologist combines. These roles may in principle be disentangled (perhaps somewhat in the Melanesian fashion), but our stubborn attempts to combine them apparently still make sense, even pay off, given the kinds of theories which tend to interest us and the sorts of ethnographic experience which have formed us, and which we cannot deny. The common aim can be stated simply enough: we want to confront the models current in the social sciences with the experiences and models of our subjects, while insisting that this should be a two-way process.

NOTE

I am grateful to Jessica Kuper, Ronald Frankenberg, Maryon McDonald, and Christina Toren for helpful comments on a draft of this introduction.

REFERENCES

Archer, Margaret S. (1988) *Culture and Agency: The Place of Culture in Social Theory*, Cambridge: Cambridge University Press.

Atran, Scott (1990) *Cognitive Foundations of Natural History: Towards an Anthropology of Science*, Cambridge: Cambridge University Press.

Bourdieu, Pierre (1972) *Esquisse d'une théorie de la pratique*, Geneva: Librairie Droz.

——(1980) *Le sens pratique*, Paris: Editions de Minuit.

Bryant, Christopher and Jary, David (eds) (1991) *Giddens' Theory of Structuration: A Critical Appreciation*, London: Routledge.

Dumont, Louis (1977) *From Mandeville to Marx: The Genesis and Triumph of Economic Ideology*, Chicago: University of Chicago Press.

——(1986) *Essays on Individualism: Modern Ideology in Anthropological Perspective*, Chicago: University of Chicago Press.

Geertz, Clifford (1988) *Works and Lives: The Anthropologist as Author*, Stanford: Stanford University Press.

Giddens, Anthony (1984) *The Constitution of Society*, Cambridge: Polity Press.

——(1990) *The Consequences of Modernity*, Cambridge: Polity Press.

Haddon, Alfred C. (1934) Second edition, *History of Anthropology*, London: Watts.

Kuper, Adam (1988) *The Invention of Primitive Society: Transformations of an Illusion*, London: Routledge.

Marett, R. R. (1927) *The Diffusion of Culture*, Cambridge: Cambridge University Press.

Part I

Individuals and networks

Chapter 1

Towards greater naturalism in conceptualizing societies

Fredrik Barth

The distinction now generally drawn in social anthropology between the connected concepts of 'society' and 'culture' was most clearly articulated by Firth:

> If . . . society is taken to be an organized set of individuals with a given way of life, culture is that way of life. If society is taken to be an aggregate of social relations, then culture is the content of those relations. Society emphasizes the human component, the aggregate of people and the relations between them. . . .
>
> (Firth 1951: 27)

Thirty years later, Leach could still write,

> In practice, 'a society' means a political unit of some sort which is territorially defined. . . . The boundaries of such units are usually vague. They are determined by operational convenience rather than rational argument. But they are objective. The members of 'a society' at any one time are a specifiable set of individuals who can be found together in one part of the map and who share common interests of some sort.
>
> (Leach 1982: 41)

Thus, while Leach, with many contemporary social anthropologists, finds the concept of culture, and especially that of cultures, highly problematic, his reservations with regard to the concept of society and societies are less strong and focus mainly on the avoidance of naive comparison between small-scale and large, complex societies.

The idea that our conceptual difficulties are found mainly on the cultural side of the antinomy, those concerning society having been more successfully resolved, may be more prevalent among anthropologists than among other social scientists. We may note Tilly's call that we 'discard the ideas of society as a thing apart and societies as overarching entities' (Tilly 1984: 17) and Wallerstein's wish to 'unthink' the whole of social science because of an unease with the way in which its object is conceptualized and partitioned (Wallerstein 1988).

Mainstream social anthropology responds to such misgivings in rather cavalier fashion. It is a commonplace that a map depicting the world as partitioned into separable, internally cohering 'societies' is a highly simplified representation of the terrain of social relations. The arbitrariness of identifying any particular level of region as a society and the embeddedness of all local regions in a world system are thereby acknowledged; yet we seem to continue the practice, and the disclaimer is not allowed to impede our comparative operations. It is also often said that 'society' should merely be regarded as short for 'social system', in the hope that this will sidestep the remaining conceptual difficulties – but observe how the term is actually used, that is, the template that it serves to evoke. Not only is the comparative project so embedded in anthropological thought that 'societies' will despite protestations be used to constitute the units of comparison but the concept of an overarching 'society' serves to *frame* our particular objects of study as if they axiomatically had to form a part of such an encompassing, larger whole. These infelicitous habits of language and conception almost invariably affirm the orderly closure that allows a holistic assumption to be applied at any level where this might seem convenient; they create the justification for a simplistic separation of endogenous and exogenous processes, and they subtly insinuate the nation-state as the implicit model for all organized human sociability.

MISCONCEPTIONS OF SOCIETY

It would probably prove tiresome and unnecessarily provocative if I were to search through anthropological texts for examples of the errors and confusions which this infelicitous use of the concept of 'society' has introduced into our theoretically intended discourse. Let us instead see what might remain of 'society' if we expunged the more patent distortions and oversimplifications which form a normal part of its content.

1. The first distortion I wish to arrest is that 'society' can be

summed up as an aggregate of social relations. If by a social relation is meant a relationship of social interaction, this does not hold. In our society, my relationships and those of others are held in place by myriad actors and agencies that I have no social dealings with but that shape my behaviour, ranging from the employees of public utilities to the organs of law and order and the branches of government. The foci of my attention and interests, and thus my activities, are further shaped by untraceable chains of intellectuals and public speakers around the world; and the options and premises for my opinions, decisions, and forging of social relations are delivered by unknown technologies and industrial concerns, buffered by the results of collective bargaining and market forces, and manipulated by mass communications. The concept of an aggregate of social relations cannot, with the utmost of goodwill, be claimed to retrieve these complex connections; and the characteristic forms of social acts and relations are not reproduced by processes which can themselves be represented as comprised of such social relations.

2. Nor can 'society' be represented as the aggregate of institutions of a population. Such a view limits social reality to its normative form and thereby resurrects the familiar difficulties of having to reintroduce informal relations besides the formal ones, deviance besides conformity to norms, and other intractable distinctions between the supposedly truly social and the additional, empirical intrusions from the supposedly non-social or anti-social.

3. Indeed, 'society' cannot defensibly be represented by *any* schema which depicts it as a whole composed of parts. Probably no such hierarchy of nesting parts within wholes will exhaust the social organization of *any* population; it can certainly not be taken as paradigmatic for all social organization. If individuals are taken to form the elementary parts, they regularly will prove to hold memberships in groups of a diversity of levels and scales and in groups which transect the boundaries of any designated region. If social statuses are seen as the minimal units, they regularly combine in overlapping structures: in corporate groups, in the status sets of reciprocal interaction, and in the composition of social persons. The complexities of social organization can neither be bounded in delimited wholes nor ordered in the unitary part–whole hierarchies which the schematism of our terminology invites us to construct.

4. Nor can these difficulties be escaped by declaring the whole world one society, a modern world system. Too many of the connections in the world are asymmetrical and indirect: decisions in a board room impinge on the life situation of an aboriginal population without that board's or its corporation's having any place in the cognized world of the population so affected or, indeed, probably vice versa. Moreover, the intersecting circles of membership and connection in the world are much older and more pervasive than the modern world system. But above all, the concept of 'society' is useful only when it helps us to identify, differentiate, and compare variations in the organization of life, not when it merges all into one unmanageable Leviathan.

5. 'Society' cannot be abstracted from the material context: all social acts are ecologically embedded. It is therefore not meaningful to separate 'society' from 'environment' and then show how the former affects or is adapted to the latter. Though the aggregate of social behaviour has a significant effect on the environment and is contained within it, social decisions on *all* levels are connected with these ecological variables and have their forms significantly affected by them. Thus the social and the ecological cannot, with respect to the forms of social events and institutions, be treated as separate systems.

6. Finally, a concept of 'society', as much as 'culture', serves to homogenize and essentialize our conception of the social. Yet we know that not only interests but also values and realities are contested between persons in stable social interaction with each other. The perfection of mutual comprehension and communication which is generally enshrined in our definition of society is not paradigmatic of social life. All social behaviour is interpreted, construed, and there is nothing to indicate that two persons ever place the same interpretation on an event. We have poor data on the degree of difference in interpretation that may obtain between regularly interacting individuals or groups. All we actually need to posit in a social relation is a degree of convergence on passing theories between the interacting persons (cf. Rorty 1989; Wikan n.d.).

In these six misconceptions I would identify the sources of the major fallacies I have noted, namely, the notions that by calling any particular area of the world a 'society' we are justified in imposing a holistic format on our description of the social organization of its population; that certain processes are endogenous to these isolates and should be understood in terms of internally shared cultural features, while others are exogenous and should be linked to culture contact, change, and modernization; and that the relevant context for human social life is everywhere a territorial unit, politically organized on the model of a nation-state.

If these fallacies are discarded, then what is left of 'society'? Something needs to be reconstituted, for to handle the materials of social anthropology we surely need a template for systems above the level of discrete social relations. But to enhance our analysis we need to revise the definitional properties with which we invest our concept of such systems. Above all, I see a need to recognize that what we have called societies are *dis*ordered systems, further characterized by an absence of closure. But how do we conceptualize and describe disordered open systems?

THE STRUCTURE OF SOCIAL ACTION

First, we need to lay a new set of foundations by updating our view of the structure of social action, taking account of the theoretical insights gained during the last twenty years.[1] Such revision will primarily need to attend to the cultural construction of reality: that human social behaviour is intended and interpreted in terms of particular cultural understandings and is not transparent, objective, and uncontested. Let us try to redescribe social action in conformity with this insight.

One possible vocabulary would distinguish two aspects of behaviour: 'events' and 'acts'. The former would refer to the outward appearance of behaviour, the objective and measurable data of positivism. The latter would refer to the intended and interpreted meaning of that behaviour, its significance for conscious persons holding particular sets of beliefs and experiences. An event is an act by virtue of being intended and construable. Leaving aside for the moment the question of epistemology, we can trace the connections of acts in two directions: back to their intent and forward to their interpretation.

The intent is the purpose of the acting person, the goal orientation from which the act sprang. This should not be confounded with the narrower question of rationality: the intent may arise as much from an urgent need to express a mood as from a clever instrumentality to achieve a specific end. Acts will generally be both instrumental in this narrower sense and expressive of the actor's orientation, condition, and position. A further tracing back to their roots leads to plans and strategies, claims to identity, and values and knowledge. The immediate output of such an intent is an event – but an event which has these properties of act to the actor.

Moving in the other direction, the event which ensues can be transformed back into an act by interpretation: a diagnosis by the onlooker as to the actor's intent but also an additional judgement of its efficacy and effect. It is thus read both as a symptom of the other and as a source of consequences. Considerable bodies of knowledge may be brought to bear by the other to achieve such an interpretation. Indeed, once the act is done, the actor may adopt a similar perspective and (re)interpret the act, revising the conception of what it really was/what really happened. And both actor and other may return over time to that question and construct novel insights into the act, in effect writing and rewriting history. The precipitate in the person of the interpretation of acts is experience and, synthetically, at a further remove, knowledge and values – which may in turn feed back on future plans and purposes as well as future interpretations of acts.

We should note that the interpretations and reinterpretations may be performed jointly, in interaction, conversation, and reminiscence with third parties. On such occasions, knowledge and cultural schemata may be transmitted from others, and further information, including estimates of reactions to the act and other consequences of it, are often brought to bear. These processes of discursive reflection will promote a convergence of understanding, knowledge, and values among those who engage in them and an enhanced focus on reality orientation in the actor.

Needless to say, the onlooker's interpretation of an act may not coincide with the actor's intent, nor will two onlookers necessarily agree in their interpretations. The event-as-act will always remain contestable and, indeed, malleable. Furthermore, the event intended and interpreted as an act will normally have a number of objective consequences in addition to, and perhaps at odds with, those intended and understood. Such consequences and entailments may in turn have important effects on the environment and on the opportunity situation of actors and others – its social consequences are in no way exhausted by a consideration of its interpretations. As noted, these further consequences can

sometimes be grasped and made accessible through the reinterpretations of actors and others – we are all capable of being
surprised by the turn of events and can reflect and learn from
this. In other words, social action generates events and chains
of consequences which are knowable and may become known:
they are not only meaningful within a framework of culturally
shaped intention and interpretation but create occasions when
people may transcend their understanding and knowledge as well
as reproduce it.

Both in conversation and in other modalities of interaction, act
and response may follow each other in rapid succession, entailing
a need for great swiftness in the interpretation of the acts of the
other. It would seem self-evident that each step of such a chain
of interaction will provide particularly useful information for the
interpretation of subsequent steps, and thus there will tend to be
a certain convergence of interpretations between the parties to
such sequences also where their interests remain distinct and their
strategies opposed. Finally, the embeddedness of all interaction in
broader social networks bears re-emphasis: one might formulate
the dictum that any social act involves minimally three parties –
me, you, and them – both in its interpretation and in its objective
consequences.

Such an account of social action seems to me to capture significant aspects of the life experience of most of us and to be
consistent with contemporary testimony in fiction and writings
in social science, if not with all of anthropology. But *if* such is
the structure of incidents of social action, this cannot but have
profound implications for the kind of systems which are formed
in social life on aggregate levels and ultimately on the level of
'society'. Particularly, I would emphasize the following:

1. Such an account does not link the social by definition to
   repetition, norms, and shared ideas as blueprints for acts and
   prerequisites for social action. On the contrary, it outlines
   interactional processes which may generate a degree of convergence, with pattern as an emergent property. I see system
   as an outcome, not as a pre-existing structure to which action
   must conform.
2. It captures a degree of disorder in that system in that it allows
   for lasting incongruities between actors, others, and third
   parties in their constructions of the meaning of events. It

allows differently positioned persons to accumulate distinctive experiences and utilize divergent schemata of interpretation: to live together in differently constructed worlds.

3. It suggests a problematic connection between the objective consequences of events and the interpreted import of events. I allow the possibility of transcending pre-established understanding, but I do not assume an empirical-realist paradigm in people's accumulation of knowledge from experience. Social consensus may indeed be the strongest factor in shaping knowledge and concepts.

4. It highlights the striking inconstancy of the import of past events which forms such an important counter-intuitive feature of contemporary views of history:[2] that acts remain eternally contestable, and their import can be rewritten.

If a multiplicity of actors were to engage repeatedly in interactions with these characteristics, what could be predicted about the resulting form? To simulate the kinds of social systems that might emerge one would need to develop rather careful theoretical deductions; but there can be little doubt that these determinants alone would predict at best a low degree of order, a perpetual flux both of the present and of people's accounts of the past, overlapping social networks with crosscutting boundaries, and an enhanced ability of parties in stable relations to agree on the interpretation of acts but no inexorable convergence towards unity and sharing of culture. In other words, it seems to depict the kinds of relations and the kind of disordered aggregate of social life that I have posited. The problem would be that it leaves social organization too underdetermined and cannot explain the degree of pattern that is regularly reported in anthropological monographs, including my own. Indeed, I would argue that this is part of its strength.

THE NEED FOR DISCOVERY PROCEDURES

Social systems vary so profoundly, both in the degree to which they are patterned and in the form and relevance which these patterns have, that a general account of social action which presupposes a particular order and form of society is necessarily suspect. Rather, we should expect that systems as disordered as those found on aggregate levels of human social life are contingent on particular historical circumstances and processes for their particular forms. This would also be consistent with what we know of objective culture history, which shows pattern and form to be continually variable and emergent. What we therefore need is not a deductive theory of what these systems will be but exploratory procedures to discover what they are: what degree of order and form they show in each particular situation in question. This needs to be discovered and described, not defined and assumed, and each system and its context should be specified in a way that will reveal the contingencies that have shaped it. Through such a procedure, we may hope to arrive at possible parameters for comparative analyses of aggregate social systems and theories about the sets of processes whereby they are generated – a singularly appropriate anthropological project.

At the initial stage of such an exploration, one certainly cannot know how to identify and circumscribe relevant units, least of all bounded societies. To place oneself in a situation where one can discover what obtains and avoid prejudging the significant scales, patterns, and foci of such disordered systems, it is advisable to start not from the top but with social actors and trace their activities and networks – to 'follow the loops', in Bateson's (1972) terms. Such a discovery procedure is admirably exemplified by Grönhaug's (1978) analysis of the Herat region of western Afghanistan.

Grönhaug's procedure consisted in pursuing the linkages of related tasks, exchanges, relationships, and material factors and thereby identifying *fields* of connected activities. He was thus able to bring out the startling discrepancies in scale between the ways activities in different fields in this particular social formation were organized and the processes whereby groups were constituted in respect to these fields. Small nucleated villages persisted through time but served essentially as way stations for a flow of passing tenant households. A 40-km-long irrigation channel of great antiquity defined an ecological unit of major scale, linking a strip of villages with a total of 100,000 inhabitants, as well as a diversity of other users (peripatetics, pastoral nomads in season, absentee landowners, a small bureaucracy of irrigation administrators) in a syndrome of joint and divided interests. With the drought in 1970–1, however, many of these relationships could be observed to change significantly. In another and separate field of activity, small-scale circles of 200–300 devotees formed around charismatic sheikhs, which proselytized, culminated, and generally moved on in regular 15–30-year cycles. Within a large geographical area with about 1,000,000 inhabitants, the town of Herat served as the central market and defined an economic and administrative region closely linked with the state through the activities of administrators, merchants, and a political and economic élite. But whereas both town and irrigation channels had functioned for over 2,000 years, the state of Afghanistan was consolidated only over the last two centuries.

'Following the loops' and mapping out the connections in 1971–2, Grönhaug linked the activities of people in the Herat area to a set of major tasks and concerns – 'fields', in his terminology. Each such field cohered as an aggregate system, showing a characteristic territorial distribution, scale, and pattern and strength of organization. But Grönhaug found no basis on which any one of these fields or any one organizational scale and territorial span could be selected to define an encompassing 'society'.

The case is directly matched by others. Following similar discovery procedures in Oman, I mapped out the town of Sohar and its close upland, an area with ca. 20,000 inhabitants (Barth 1983). The population belongs to five different ethnic and linguistic groups, with broad and discrepant distributions into Arabia, Iran, Baluchistan, Sind, and Gujarat, respectively. These ethnic groups practice different customs – some of them intriguingly reversing each other, others merely contrasting in ways that exhibit no logical articulation. The complex social strata and classes of Sohar likewise participate in separate and discrepant circles and regions – merchants orienting themselves towards trading towns in the whole Gulf area and towards Bombay, civil servants looking to the capital in Muscat, Bedouin aligning in tribes with home areas in the mountains and in the Empty Quarter, labour migrants commuting to Kuwait, Qatar, and Abu Dhabi, and fishermen narrowly focusing on zones and sectors of the local sea and fish auctions on the beach. The religious affiliations of local congregations of worship divide the population in terms of another set of four distinct identities – Sunni, Shiite, Ibadhi, and Hindu – of which only the last coincides with any of the other groupings. All in all, the absence of any encompassing single and whole 'society' and the crosscutting of connections in multiple directions over large regions proves even more striking than in the Herat area.

Another aspect of this intersecting, multicentric condition is that the religious communities represented in Sohar live interspersed, their members dealing with members of all the other groups in work, leisure, and as fellow citizens; yet these parties to interaction will embrace different dogmas, cosmologies, bodies of law, and current positions on morality, culture, and politics – positions which are, moreover, continually in flux. These premises and positions are all being developed and articulated in distant and different metropolitan centres – Mecca, Cairo, Teheran, Qom, Nizwa in Inner Oman – by persons wrapped up in other lives and problems than those of Soharis. Yet their various edicts and announcements carry powerful theological, moral, and social authority among the respective sectors of the town's population. A major source of disorder is thereby injected and replenished in the small town of Sohar from a multiplicity of different sources. Could one ever expect its population to have the capacity to process these ideas and the multiplicity of others arising within and without and create the integration, order, and unity which features in the conventional definition of society? What might the institutions and processes look like that could produce such feats of society-building?

The weak concept of 'negotiation', which is now often introduced to suggest how interpersonal encounters are handled, falls far short of this challenge. 'Negotiation' suggests a degree of conflict of interests but within a framework of shared understandings. The disorder entailed in the religious, social, ethnic, class, and cultural pluralism of Sohar goes far beyond what can be retrieved as ambiguities of interest, relevance, and identity and resolved by negotiation. What is more, I am struck by the questionable relevance of many of the ideological flotsam to the cognized and objective life situations of the parties who indeed adopt them: What sense can new signals out of Teheran make of the life situation of a Shiite widow in Sohar? How might the successional conflicts of the early Caliphate which defined the schism between Sunnis and Ibadhis illuminate the condition of a young Ibadhi man today? These do not arise from local interests that people pursue, they introduce perplexities that may confound their lives. Yet these are the ideas they respectively embrace, in terms of which they live with each other and try to make sense of their lives. The result is no doubt a system of a kind (in that Soharis come to know each other and interact), and it should be describable; but it must in truth be a *dis*ordered system, very different from the textbook definition of 'society', and one in which convergence takes place through many processes other than 'negotiation'.

We need to identify these processes and model their parameters and results, and we need to redesign our whole thinking about 'society' accordingly. These are pervasive problems and issues which impinge deeply and broadly on the kind of theory anthropology needs for its tasks. The lesson becomes even clearer if we reflect on the issue of how society appears over time – for example, what has happened in Herat since Grönhaug did his first study and analysis (cf. Grönhaug n.d.). Because of ideological and social clashes in a small élite and massive foreign interference, a coup was precipitated in Kabul and swiftly followed by another and by the Soviet invasion. These events delegitimated the central and provincial authorities in Herat, though the population there had played little part in the events and conflicts of interest that led up to the events. In 1980 Herat became one of the first sites of large-scale resistance fighting (Klass 1987). Since then, perhaps as much as one-third of the population has sought refuge elsewhere, land-use patterns have changed drastically, supplies and trade have sought new paths into Iran, and Mujahid commanders have emerged as the key political leaders, aligned in different, loose factions under various international patronage (Saudi, Iranian, Pakistani, US).

These are not simply changes that have been imposed on the population: they are the active response of people to the dramatic changes of circumstances. People have *responded* by rising against the government, developing an unprecedented political organization, fleeing and creating networks and activities in new localities, etc. These results can be described as emergent systems, probably with a low degree of order; they have been generated through ambiguous and innovative interactions between strangers and old acquaintances struggling to interpret new circumstances and each other's acts and forging tentative and constantly provisional understandings and relationships.

The template of an encompassing society organizing a shared way of life seemed to have little to contribute towards an understanding of Herat in 1972, and it is even less useful to represent this situation of the 1980s. But if we also ask such a template to straddle the twenty years from 1970 till today, its inadequacy becomes outrageous: it can shed no useful light on the social events that have unfolded and exhibited pattern and meaning and connection during these years. Yet there can be no doubt that there has been not only ephemeral pattern but also significant continuity in Herat through these years – not only meaning but also values, organization, institutions, long-term strategies, cooperation, and concerted efforts to create a degree of order in social life, all the features supposedly characterizing society. A template which fails so utterly in a situation in which some of the usual parameters change cannot be retained as a key foundation for general theory.

THE STRUCTURE OF LOCAL COMMUNITIES

It relieves none of the pressure on the received concept of society to argue that the phenomena I have discussed are uniquely characteristic of particular societies of the Middle East or of the breakdown connected with modern warfare or of modernization. No doubt all three arguments could be sustained for particular features of the materials discussed, but this would not provide a basis for declaring them irrelevant to a general social theory. Moreover, similar, analogous, or equally problematic materials can be marshalled from other areas of the world with which I am familiar and from situations that are 'traditional' as well as under clearly modern circumstances.

What, then, of anthropology's most favoured materials: those from primitive and pristine areas? Is anthropology's model of society perhaps adequate and defensible for such communities, and thus appropriate for the original condition of mankind and for elementary forms of society, though perhaps not directly applicable to later, more complex developments? And do we not, in most populations of mankind, still find the *Gemeinschaften* of local communities which, despite exogenous forces which impinge on them, largely recreate these fundamental conditions of sociability?

I would argue, to the contrary, that the anthropological construct of the local community is itself a stifling, pervasive artifact of the traditional anthropological fiction of society, which has often perverted our understanding and representation of the realities of life in small communities and prevented the anthropological fieldworker from noticing, exploring, depicting, and drawing the required conclusions from evidence which is pervasively accessible.

Indeed, I believe it could be shown that the anthropological development of the 'community-study method' as a format for fieldwork in Western and traditional civilizations was a symptom of this same insistence. Rather than being simply a way to capitalize in large-scale societies on a valuable fieldwork methodology based on participant observation (which could have been achieved by other means), it served as a desperate attempt to salvage the simplicity of an inadequate concept of society in the face of unwelcome contrary materials (cf. Arensberg 1961).

But how about those local communities of tribal groups that have provided the basic paradigm for anthropological theoretical constructions: do they exhibit the integrated and holistic features supposedly characterizing 'society'? A careful reading of the corpus of Firth's work on Tikopia (see esp. Firth 1964) goes a long way towards arresting such simple stereotypes and shows the variables of positioning, contests of interpretation, and diversities of values, knowledge, and orientation in a community as small and insulated as any in the world.

No doubt, the fact of lifelong co-membership in a small and often highly interdependent and cooperating group will have an effect on the conditions of interaction, the character of social relations, and the sharing of knowledge and values. But these should be studied as the effects of those exceptional conditions of small scale and isolation, not as the paradigm for living in society! Specifically, I would suggest that the degree of order in social interactions and relations, the degree of sharing of culture, and the adequacy of mutual interpretations are questions which can be studied in a local community and are potentially discoverable, that they are variables which represent the effects of processes which can be identified and studied, and that such studies would produce new insights of importance to basic social theory.

Why, in all the work of ethnography, have such questions been given so little attention? We have finally over the last two decennia obtained some knowledge of gender differences in culture within small-scale communities, but these data have been collected for other reasons and used for other purposes than those I am suggesting. We have been aware of differences in specialized functions, expertise, and secret knowledge, but the main disciplinary concern has been to translate this into advice on how to find the best-informed informants. What of the striking differences in interests which we must all have noticed during fieldwork between persons of the same gender and generation? How do they arise, how do they affect interaction, and what are

their other implications? What about the deep scepticism about
the beliefs and conventions of tribal culture that distinguishes
occasional members of primitive communities? How are such
awesome intellectual independence and powers developed, and
what do they reveal about the connection between belief and
social action? What are the frequencies and the entailments of
biculturalism in traditional tribal contexts? Indeed, what are the
effects of local exogamy on social interaction, and what degree of
cultural pluralism and dynamism does it engender?

Rather than accumulate data on what are probably profound
variations in such matters and use the data to generate social
theory, anthropologists seem to have been happier simply to
reaffirm Tönnies (1940). I see three possible reasons this has
been so. First, no doubt our understanding is often so unsubtle
and our data so crude that they cannot distinguish what, compared
with our ignorance of tribal life and culture, appear as mere
differences in nuance. Perhaps also, our materials are often so
thin that it is only by combining them all in one homogenized
account that we are able to give an appearance of coverage.
Secondly, anthropology has been pursued in colonial situations
or in the recent context of new nations. This circumstance may
disingenuously have been used to provide trash cans for unwanted
data: all links beyond the local community could be ignored as
distortions and dilutions of a pristine state of cultural purity and
homogeneity. Behind the above, however, I sense a fear of the
destruction of a simple template of 'society', with the loss of
innocence and the frightening enlargement of ethnographic and
analytic tasks that would entail. To be able to say something about
the *degree* of order, to characterize disordered and unbounded
systems, and to read action and interpretation in a foreign culture
with sufficient subtlety to record individual differences, we need to
proceed with greater precision, better method, and more justified
confidence than we are accustomed to muster. Yet, the rewards of
attempting it are within our reach and will put our analyses on a
better footing.

The way to proceed is clearly indicated. If we wish to make our
concept of 'society' useful to our analysis of social relations and
social institutions as they are manifest in the actions of people,
we need to think of society as the context of actions and results of
actions but not as a *thing* – or it will persist as an ossified object in
the body of our developing social theory. The recognition of social

positioning and multiple voices simply invalidates any account of society as a shared set of ideas enacted by a population. Realizing that ideas, considerations, and intentions differ among interacting persons, we need to adopt a perspective that allows us to model the resulting processes, the disordered systemic properties that are thereby generated, and the pervasive flux that ensues. A continued use, on the other hand, of the received templates of society as a bounded and ordered entity and of local communities as exemplary parts of such an entity will only continue to mystify our data and trivialize our results.

NOTES

1 Talcott Parsons's classic formulation (1937) dominated thinking until about 1970, and it still seems to survive in the anthropologists' idea of society. The theoretical breakthrough that provides a new perspective may be identified with the publications of Berger and Luckman (1966) and Geertz (1973).
2 Cf. Wallerstein – 'the past is so frequently and so rapidly reformulated and revised that it seems almost evanescent at times' (1988: 531) – and Colson – 'we have found people revising their memories as they tailor their ideas about the appropriate ordering of their society to their experience of the compromises involved in daily lives' (1984: 6).

REFERENCES

Anderson, B. (1983) *Imagined Communities: Reflections on the Origin and Spread of Nationalism*, London: Verso.
Arensberg, C. (1961) 'The community as object and as sample', *American Anthropologist* 63: 241–63.
Barth, F. (1983) *Sohar: Culture and Society in an Omani Town*, Baltimore: Johns Hopkins University Press.
Bateson, G. (1972) *Steps to an Ecology of Mind*, New York: Ballantine.
Berger, P. L. and Luckman, T. (1966) *The Social Construction of Reality*, Harmondsworth: Penguin.
Colson, E. (1984) 'The reordering of experience: anthropological involve-ment with time', *Journal of Anthropological Research* 40: 1–13.
Firth, R. (1951) *Elements of Social Organization*, London: Watts.
——(1964) *Essays on Social Organization and Values*, London: Athlone Press.
Geertz, C. (1973) *The Interpretation of Cultures*, New York: Basic Books.
Grönhaug, R. (1978) 'Scale as a variable in analysis: fields in social organization in Herat, north-west Afghanistan', in F. Barth (ed.) *Scale and Social Organization*, Oslo: Universitetsforlaget.
——(n.d.) 'Herati people reconstructing their lifeworld', MS.

Klass, R. (ed.) (1987) *Afghanistan: The Great Game Revisited*, New York: Freedom House.

Leach, E. R. (1982) *Social Anthropology*, Glasgow: Fontana.

Parsons, T. (1937) *The Structure of Social Action*, Glencoe: Free Press.

Rorty, R. (1989) *Contingency, Irony, and Solidarity*, Cambridge: Cambridge University Press.

Tilly, C. (1984) *Big Structures, Large Processes, Huge Comparisons*, New York: Russell Sage Foundation.

Tönnies, F. (1940) *Fundamental Concepts of Society*, trans. and ed. C. Loomis, New York: American Book Co.

Wallerstein, I. (1988) 'Should we unthink nineteenth-century social science?', *International Social Science Journal* 118: 527.

Wikan, U. (n.d.) 'Beyond the words: the power of resonance', *American Ethnologist* (in press).

Chapter 2

The global ecumene as a network of networks

Ulf Hannerz

A half-century has now passed since Radcliffe-Brown published his paper 'On Social Structure' (1940). In that paper, he wrote (taking Australian Aborigines as his example) that 'these human beings are connected by a complex network of social relations', and for that 'network of actually existing relations' he proposed to use the term 'social structure'. It is to the idea of networks of social relationships that I will return here – even though that idea has gone through changes since then, the context will be very different, and my ultimate concern, in a disgracefully un-Radcliffe-Brownian manner, is actually with culture.

The ethnographic context I have in mind is the world.[1] In the twentieth century, and particularly in its latter half, that entity has become increasingly one and indivisible in ways without direct earlier parallels. Large-scale administration, commerce, and industry have imposed a certain amount of uniformity at some levels, but globalization is also a matter of increasing coherence, a pattern of intensified transnational contacts. The transport technology of this century has made it possible to move about quickly over greater distances than ever before. And when people themselves do not move, communication media now allow the long-distance passage of uniquely varied kinds of meaning and meaningful form.

We are now surely also exposed to never-ending commentary on this present and a future expected to bring more of the same – the rhetoric of globalbabble, as one commentator has aptly put it.[2] My purpose here is not to add to globalbabble at its customary high level of generality. As a part of an ongoing effort to explore what social anthropology can credibly contribute to the understanding of contemporary global or transnational cultural processes by way of an orderly build-up of ethnography and analysis, I want to consider a little more specifically a few problem areas in which network concepts may be of some use to our anthropological imagination. Before embarking on this undertaking, however, let me sketch some background assumptions and cite some relevant history of anthropological ideas.

THE GLOBAL ECUMENE, THE STUDY OF CIVILIZATIONS, AND THE GROWTH OF NETWORK ANALYSIS

By and large, the response of anthropologists to the intensifying process of world integration may have been most visible at two levels, and the intellectual context in which it may now be of some interest to reconsider network ideas has two major aspects which seem to relate to these levels, in one case directly and in the other perhaps more indirectly.

On the one hand, there has been the task of illuminating the influence of wider structures, usually of alien origin, on local life mostly in non-Western peripheral regions. The recent tendency here has been to acknowledge the power of such expansive structures to transform local social and cultural forms but also to suggest the vitality and creativity of local responses – often described in terms of a perhaps too undifferentiated notion of 'resistance'. On the other hand, there has been that part of the experimentation in anthropological writing, especially among our American colleagues, which has to do, they say, with a decline of ethnographic authority; if the anthropologist was once in fairly undisputed control at the Checkpoint Charlies between what were at least depicted as bounded cultures, with globalization the walls come tumbling down and our voices are perhaps only heard within a chorus or a cacophony.

With respect to the former of these concerns, we can now sense a growing dissatisfaction with the ways in which wider frameworks have rather offhandedly been brought into ethnographies. Sally Falk Moore (1986: 329 ff.), for example, has criticized that variety of 'two-system model' in which only the extremes of scale, the largest and the smallest, are considered and are linked largely by theoretical formulae. In the same vein, the prominent commentator on anthropological writing George Marcus (1989: 8) has recently noted the risk of relying on varieties of macrotheory which, in the form in which anthropologists pick them up, may be about to become obsolete within their own research traditions, where one is now moving 'in a less totalistic, more pluralistic direction – one more open to decentralized, mutable ideas of structure'.[3]

The other aspect of the current situation in anthropological thinking which I have in mind is one which brings the task of conceptualizing society particularly close to that of understanding culture. This is the growing recognition that culture theory needs to be enhanced by a sociology of knowledge – that structures of meaning and meaningful form are not uniformly shared but problematically distributed in populations and that both culture itself and the order of social relationships are significantly influenced by this distributive complexity (see, e.g., Wallace 1961; Goodenough 1971; Schwartz 1978a, b; Barth 1987: 77; 1989; Keesing 1987; Hannerz 1980: 280 ff.; 1982; 1983: 157 ff.; 1986: 363; 1987: 550 ff.; 1989a; 1992). Such understandings have grown out of varied sources, and the experiences of globalization make up only one of these. Yet the affinity between the sense of loss of ethnographic authority and the increasing emphasis on distributive views of culture can be sensed in the recent popularity of terms such as 'polyphony', 'heteroglossia', and 'plurivocality'.

The implication of Moore's and Marcus's criticisms seems to be that anthropologists should devote more of their own energy to issues of macroanalysis and micro–macro connections. And while the social organization of meaning may well be more intricate even in small-scale social units than classical as well as much recent interpretive anthropology has made it out to be, the distributive problematic becomes more obvious in any attempt to construct a macroanthropology. This is my point of departure here. Marcus (1989: 24–5), in that recent article to which I have just referred, takes notice of some papers of mine which 'attempt to define a construct of world, rather than local culture', and concludes, generously enough I think, that while my 'definition of the space of cultural process is eloquent and clear, it is difficult to know how this conceptualization relates to strategies of ethnographic research and writing'. I am afraid I cannot now provide anything like a final and comprehensive response to this comment. At this point, in any case, anthropologists are probably better off behaving like foxes rather than hedgehogs in looking for ways to deal with larger-scale structures – that is, exploring many perhaps partial and complementary approaches rather than hoping to find the one big solution. In that spirit, however, I would like to sketch some ways in which network notions may offer a vocabulary for formulating personal and ethnographic experiences and intuitions concerning contemporary cultural organization in a relatively disciplined way, rather than entirely, however brilliantly, *ad hoc*, with some potential for further development and increased precision. Perhaps in the context of this volume I can be forgiven if this will involve rather relentless conceptualizing and not much ethnography.

I discern a usable past for the kind of macroanthropology of culture I have in mind in the rather tentative writings by Kroeber, Redfield, and a number of other scholars often in some way connected to the latter, on conceptions of civilization. This is mostly midcentury work, but one may see it as part of anthropology's unfinished business, left behind at some point, along with so much else, as research interests in the discipline have twisted and turned, but also still there to be retrieved and rethought (leaving aside some well-known Kroeberian and Redfieldian proclivities which we need not harp on here).

Referring to the world in its state of relative cohesion as a global ecumene, and concerning myself especially with its cultural dimensions, I draw some inspiration from Alfred Kroeber's 1945 Huxley Memorial Lecture to the Royal Anthropological Institute, discussing the ecumene of the ancient Greeks. That ecumene, the total inhabited world as the Greeks understood it, was a smaller one, stretching from Gibraltar towards India and a rather uncertainly perceived China. Resurrecting the notion now on the basis of a more current understanding of globality, I would agree with Kroeber (1945: 9) both that it 'remains a convenient designation for an interwoven set of happenings and products which are significant equally for the culture historian and the theoretical anthropologist' – which, incidentally, I do not necessarily take to be entirely separate vocations – and that

> while any national or tribal culture may and must for certain purposes be viewed and analyzed by itself . . . any such culture is necessarily in some degree an artificial unit segregated off for expediency and . . . the ultimate natural unit for ethnologists is 'the culture of all humanity at all periods and in all places'.

The concept of the global ecumene, all this goes to say, connects some concerns of the present to an anthropological research tradition, albeit a minority one; it poses a contrast to that basic assumption of a global mosaic which underlies so much anthropology and which has long allowed us to be rather neglectful of the need to develop a macroanthropology; and it may, finally, be an alternative to the concept of 'world system', which, for all its obvious attractions, has perhaps already become too fraught with surplus theoretical and ideological baggage which we may be unwilling to take on – including a rather limited understanding of culture.[4]

In other ways, it is rather the work of Redfield and his associates and followers – among whom, in this particular context, I would include Singer, Cohn, and Marriott – that I see as providing the useful antecedents for my purposes. As Milton Singer (1972: 254) has pointed out, while 'Kroeber's cultural historical approach . . . is telescopic, diachronic, and cultural, Redfield's starting point was microscopic, synchronic, and sociocultural', although from there he went on 'to develop ideas for a social anthropological study of civilizations that is macroscopic and historical' (see also Singer 1976, 1988).

In his work on the characteristics of small communities, Redfield showed his familiarity with the relevant contemporary European scholarship, and in this connection he made reference also to that study of the Norwegian parish of Bremnes by John Barnes (1954), which – setting aside the occasional early formulation such as Radcliffe-Brown's – is generally understood to have been the beginning of more organized interest in social networks in anthropology (cf. Redfield 1956: 25 ff.; 1962: 385). And, in one way or other, network understandings soon also figured prominently in that collective Chicago-based research enterprise devoted to Indian civilization which Redfield had a part in initiating. There is, not least, Marriott and Cohn's 'Networks and Centres in the Integration of Indian Civilization' (1958), in which the overall sociocultural pattern of India is seen as organized on the one hand by widespread, diffuse networks of trade, marriage, politics, and religion and on the other hand by a multiplicity of centres distinguished at many levels of greater or lesser scope without any neat hierarchy and functioning in relationship to the networks just mentioned. Such networks may be found in every civilization, Marriott and Cohn argue, but their high development may have been indispensable to the looseness and variety characteristic of the integration of Indian society and culture. And the centres, even as they organized the cultural diversity of the whole, contributed to it through their internal cultural processes. In another paper from the same period, Marriott (1959) discusses tendencies of change in the channels of cultural transmission in India. Print media, broadcasting, and new means of transportation, he suggests here, upset some of the old tangled networks and cut out centres at intermediate levels, and 'a map of the Indian railroads may thus become a better guide to the sacred geography of the emerging India than any painstaking research into the epic wanderings of Ram and the Pandavas' (Marriott 1959: 72).

While network ideas thus had a part in the beginning macro-anthropological conceptualization of Indian civilization and of civilizations more generally, it is obvious that close attention to the formal properties of networks increased during a slightly later period, in other intellectual and ethnographic settings. Barnes's Norwegian study and Bott's (1957) study of English families pioneered a more specialized concern with network ideas, but particularly in the late 1960s and early 1970s a conspicuous number of studies drew on this and related concepts in analysing such matters as informal social control, micropolitics, and manipulations in the pursuit of resources.[5]

Again, anthropology moved on, and at the frontiers of anthropological thought in recent years hardly anyone has paid much attention to networks (at the same time as 'network' may have come into increasing use in the ordinary vocabulary and 'networking' as a verb and a conscious activity has become fashionable in some circles of Western societies).[6] In retrospect, one can see why. Generally, this wave of network anthropology was linked to action and exchange theories and prototheories which soon went out of fashion. Formal network analysis of the intensity which some favoured could only be carried out in very small units, at least if it were to be based on observational data as was suggested, and it thus became extremely microsociological. When any greater slice of social reality was contemplated, data threatened to become quickly very unwieldy.[7] The methodological problems we sense here have helped lead network studies towards becoming one more (computer-aided) social science specialty but now, it would seem, with fewer anthropologists involved. A further fact concerning network studies in the period I have just referred to is that they were mostly preoccupied with social morphology and with the management of material and power resources, while on the whole they had little to say about culture. And since structures of meaning and meaningful form have lately been the focus of attention of much anthropology, even to the exclusion of sociological concerns, there may have seemed to be little of any use in network thinking. In this, however, these studies differed from the Redfield-inspired work on Indian civilization.

OPENNESS AND INCLUSIVENESS

For my present purposes, what above all makes network analysis attractive is its openness. As Srinivas and Béteille (1964: 165–6) have pointed out, again in an Indian context, 'the concept of social network paves the way to an understanding of the linkage existing between different institutional spheres and between different systems of groups and categories'. Moreover, a network 'ramifies in every direction, and, for all practical purposes, stretches out indefinitely. . . .' Networks, that is, can be seen to cut across more conventional units of analysis.

The rationale for bringing network concepts into cultural analysis is that in complex cultures especially, different meanings and meaningful forms may occur in different social relationships and that, at the same time, apart from whatever may be the respective internal dynamics of these relationships, the cultural contents of more or less adjacent relationships may impinge on one another. That is, there is a significant distributive problematic that we may map in network terms. It is true that cultural processes work in large part through a rather high degree of redundancy, in which there are few privileged moments and few entirely unique social relationships, but there is still enough social differentiation of these processes to make it worthwhile to distinguish a range of typical loci and recurrent sequences. Particularly important for a perspective towards the cultural organization of the global ecumene, too, networks allow us, as we follow them, to escape the constraints of place characteristic of most ethnographic formats. When culture as a collective phenomenon is understood to belong primarily to social relationships and their networks and only derivatively and without logical necessity to particular territories, then we can see how it is nowadays organized in the varied connections between the local and the long-distance.

What I want to do now is to point to three areas, certainly in themselves closely interconnected, in which a sense of network forms can help us delineate characteristic cultural processes of the global ecumene. One of them has to do with the diversification of individual agency in the social organization of meaning. Another

involves the variety of parallel but different connections between
territorially anchored cultures which is a conspicuous feature of
the twentieth-century world. The third relates to the usefulness
of seeing the large-scale organization of culture in a step-by-step
fashion in extended series of relationships.

Before getting into these matters, however, I must draw attention to the fact that the more intensive network analyses of the
late 1960s and early 1970s took a quite limited view of which
kinds of relationships were to be included in their studies. These
were personal networks not only in the explicit sense of being,
frequently, ego-centred; they also tended to be viewed as con-
sisting only of personal relationships in which the participants
were familiar to one another as individuals, engaging largely
in face-to-face encounters. It is symptomatic that as far as the
handling of information was concerned, the most frequent topic
of these studies was gossip, the microcultural stuff of small-scale
milieux where socially organized meanings attached to particular
individuals, events, and settings.[8] But meaning, in the contemporary world, flows in no small part within frameworks organized by
state and market; it also flows between people who are strangers to
each other, and it moves not only through face-to-face contacts but
through the cultural technology of the media as well. If one wants
to draw on network thinking in attempts to understand culture and
cultural process, then, one can either stick to a concentration on
personal relationships – but in that case one has to be aware of how
much is left out of the picture – or expand the coverage to include
(in principle, although certainly not in every case in practice) all
the relationships, all the channels, in which productions of meaning
and the interpretation of those productions occur.

For the purpose of a macroanthropology, the latter, more inclusive alternative is preferable. There is a need here for one coherent
yet flexible language of form for social relationships and the
relationships between relationships – a conceptualization which
can cover varying degrees of symmetry and asymmetry in social
organization, not least with regard to scale and directedness. In
this I prefer to differ to some extent also from the usage of Marriott
and Cohn in their distinction between networks and centres in the
organization of Indian civilization. They appear to reserve the term
'network' for sets of relationships which exhibit a relatively high
degree of symmetry – that is, reciprocity – in what I take to be a
largely spontaneous, not very reflective flow of meaning which is

an integral part of a more or less quotidian conduct of relationships transcending the local scene. Their 'centres', in contrast, are local concentrations of people engaging in characteristically asymmetrical external relationships with people normally residing elsewhere – asymmetrical both in the sense of scale, as relatively few cultural specialists have much the same kinds of relationships to relatively many, and in the sense of directionality, as the flow of meaning is understood to be more from centre to periphery than vice versa. The distinction is no doubt useful, but rather than relying on just those two not-quite-matching concepts and seeing them in terms of polarity, one may discern that networks may include relationships of varying degrees and kinds of symmetry or asymmetry.

THE NETWORK OF PERSPECTIVES

In much ethnographic as well as theoretical writing, of course, the issue of individual agency in cultural analysis hardly appears (Hannerz 1992 esp. chap. 3; n.d.a.). On the whole, the culture concept in anthropology has been unreflectively sociocentric. The nature of the collectiveness of 'collective representations' is not often made a matter for inquiry, nor are the variations in organization covered by that general notion scrutinized. This rather easygoing handling of a central idea may be serviceable enough in the prototypical small-scale society, in which people exposed to much the same living conditions have similar personal experiences and are at the same time available to a massively redundant communication flow only from people largely like themselves. There is, on the whole, one network of uniformly rather high density. Under such circumstances, just possibly, what are individual constructions and what received transmissions perhaps in the end makes little difference.[9] The ideal formula for the social organization of meaning, from the individual's point of view, becomes 'I know, and I know that everyone else knows, and I know that everyone else knows that I know', and so forth.

In a more complex situation, it becomes increasingly obvious that the individual's perspective, the individual's share or version of socially organized meaning, is in large part a product of his network experience, and that the greater variety and the less density there is in ego-centred networks, the more different perspectives will be. It would also seem to follow that the more socially

differentiated and even individualized will be the management
of meaning within these perspectives (for a related formulation
see Coser 1975). There will tend to be greater variation in the
way in which different experiences, different flows of meaning, are
weighted relative to one another and in the way they are brought
together or, for that matter, compartmentalized. The probability
that institutionalized solutions for such management problems will
be available appears smaller. And as the individual has to cope
rather more independently with gaps and contradictions in the
cultural materials coming his way, there may be a growth in what
can be termed metacultural sensibilities. Individuals' perspectives,
then, come to consist of the conceptions which they have come to
construct or appropriate for their own use, as it were, but also
of their perspectives on other perspectives – their approximate
mappings of other people's meanings. And culture as a collective
phenomenon becomes the network of such perspectives.

So far this is a rather abstract formulation. For something more
concrete, let me refer to my colleague Tomas Gerholm's (1988)
brief interpretive essay on three European intellectual converts
to Islam: the turn-of-the-century Swedish painter Ivan Aguéli,
who became Abdul Hadi al-Maghrabi, the Polish-Jewish journalist
Leopold Weiss, who became Muhammad Asad in the 1920s, and
the French Communist Party theoretician Roger Garaudy, who,
about a decade ago, became Raja Garoudi.[10] Gerholm shows how
these three converts conducted their post-conversion cultural work
in contrasting ways, which appear to have been based in part on
different network positions. Aguéli, an itinerant artist who traveled
in the Middle East and India and spent much of his time in Paris,
was only Abdul Hadi in an on-and-off way and as a matter of
degree – more when he was among fellow Muslims away from
Europe, less when he was in those bohemian circles in Paris
where his Muslim faith, if it was known, was only seen as one
of his several eccentricities. And he was more Muslim than ever,
it seems, when Abdul Hadi became the pen name of a publicist,
a religious propagandist who never let on in his writing that he was
actually a European convert. Garaudy has also remained largely
outside the Islamic community. Within it his conversion has been
seen to legitimate the general superiority of the Muslim faith, even
as his personal influence has remained very limited; he has been a
betwixt-and-between intellectual, engaging different civilizational
currents in dialogue. Only Weiss really became Muhammad Asad,

moving more fully from a Western to an Islamic network. And speaking from a position well within the latter, he could draw effectively on the whole range of his experiences, as his loyalty was in no doubt.

Some years ago, in an attempt to work out the variations in urban personal networks, I distinguished three main tendencies, which I termed encapsulation, segregativity, and integrativity (Hannerz 1980: 255 ff.).[11] Turning to a network conceptualization of culture and to differences in the management of meaning, I sense that the same distinctions may be useful. To reiterate, there are people who remain within networks in which largely the same or closely related meanings and meaningful forms reach them through all relationships and they in turn play their part in keeping these meanings and forms in continued circulation. In contrast, there are those whose networks put them in touch with various quite divergent cultural sets – not least through their long-distance relationships. A basic distinction here may be drawn between a tendency to keep these cultural sets apart, engaging with them in different relationships but segregating them, and a tendency to integrate them, to bring the cultural content of one sector of one's network more directly and perhaps overtly to bear on the management of meaning in another sector – perhaps even set up additional network relationships by which the sectors come into direct contact.

No doubt there are all kinds of intermediate forms between these types. It seems to me, however, that in Aguéli's personal management of meaning, there is more of segregativity, of compartmentalization. Garaudy is apparently engaged in one kind of integrativity. Weiss/Muhammad Asad's case may suggest even more clearly than the other two that time may need to be incorporated into network analyses; his management of meaning can perhaps be seen, with some simplification, as one biographically constituted by the passage from one phase of relative encapsulation to another.

In the context of the global ecumene, the emphasis on culture as a social organization of perspectives suggests that not only do perspectives differ depending on from where one sees things; one may also see variously far. With different perspectives go different horizons. Some people, like Aguéli, Garaudy, and Weiss, are much more involved in long-distance, even transnational contacts than others. The familiar dichotomy between cosmopolitans and locals only begins to draw attention to the variations here.[12] I have suggested elsewhere that the cosmopolitan in a narrow sense is perhaps a compartmentalizer, someone who wants separate cultures to be separate and relishes the differences between them. This would be in some contrast, then, to those who engage more systematically in cultural integrativity – in syntheses, in syncretism, in what under some conditions I would refer to as creolization.[13] But there can be further variations here in the way that social and cultural dimensions are interrelated. Even in the present-day phase of globalization, of course, a great many people are, if not fully, at least to a greater extent encapsulated within local, face-to-face contexts where largely sociocentric notions of culture may suffice for analytical purposes. Yet at least in limited, perhaps piecemeal ways their perspectives, too, reach beyond local communities, and their networks may include others whose horizons are quite different.

PARALLEL CONNECTIONS

Thinking in network terms, I have just suggested, may help us realize how issues of differentiated and individuated agency become more prominent in cultural analysis in some social conditions than in others. My second concern is the multiplicity of more or less parallel linkages through which globalization now occurs. Let me quickly summarize how major perspectives towards global integration have dealt with questions of culture.

On the one hand, research inspired by world-system theory has tended to emphasize how local cultures become more or less radically reconstructed in ideological or practically adaptive response to the imposition of new frameworks of power and material production.[14] This research often deals with periods of early European expansion or climactic colonialism, and thus it depicts periods in which growing external constraints on political and material life were still combined with some relative autonomy in the local management of meaning.

On the other hand, a mass of documentation and commentary has been preoccupied with that transnational diffusion of culture which is so conspicuous in present times – particularly by way of the mass media and commoditized popular culture, mostly from North America to the rest of the world – and which is often seen as a threat to the survival of cultural diversity (see, e.g., Schiller

1976, Hamelinck 1983, Mattelart 1983). In extreme asymmetry in terms of directedness and scale, the media especially allow the few to reach the many, in impressive micro-to-macro leaps, while providing at most for limited and meagre feedback. Perhaps the scholarly engagement with such matters has never yet been elevated to the level of prestigious theory, and anthropologists have in large part ignored them, but the imagery of massive diffusion is certainly nowadays ever available to anyone offering as much as a passing thought to the globalization of culture.

The different emphases of these two bodies of writing both give some considerable insight into the cultural processes of a world becoming more integrated; one should be aware that to some degree they point in contrasting directions, as one shows how the world system becomes more culturally differentiated through a global division of labour while the other suggests homogenization. What neither the emphasis on the political economy of cultural reconstruction in the world-system periphery nor the preoccupation with dramatic large-scale diffusion really attends to, however, is the great proliferation in the twentieth century of transnational linkages more reminiscent of what Marriott and Cohn in their delineation of Indian civilization identified as networks. The things that matter more here are on the one hand the many varieties of travel and on the other hand all those varieties of media which are not *mass* media – photography, tape recordings, the telephone, the fax, the computer, and the good old-fashioned personal letter, all employed in fairly symmetrical relationships with regard to scale and directionality – and also those which are asymmetrical to a degree without being 'mass': specialized books and journals.

Without travel and the non-mass media, we would not have a wide range of ethnic diasporas, transnational corporations, jet set and brain drain, tourism, charter flight *hajj* and other modern pilgrimages, invisible colleges in science, exchange students, au pair girls, foreign pen pals as part of growing up, transcontinental families, international aid bureaucracies, summer beach parties of backpacking Interrail-pass-holders from all over, and among voluntary associations everything from Amnesty International to the European Association of Social Anthropologists. It is these dispersed institutions and communities, groupings of people regularly coming together and moving apart, short-term relationships or patterns of fleeting encounter, which offer the contexts in which globalization occurs as the personal experience of a great many people in networks where extremely varied meanings flow. These networks are indeed denser in some parts of the world than in others, but they are hardly now a feature only of Western industrial society. It is in no small part because of them that anthropologists increasingly have to worry about ethnographic authority. And just as Marriott and Cohn suggested that the overall pattern of Indian civilization was typically one of looseness and internal diversity to which the variety of networks was fundamental, the same may now well be said about the twentieth-century global ecumene.

The first thing to say about these various networks is that while we are well aware of their existence, we have little organized knowledge about most of them. Tourism by now has its ethnographers, but most of the other phenomena in this domain do not. To call them all networks can perhaps not be very wrong, but it is obvious that the quality of the social linkages of which they are composed is far from all the same, ranging rather from close personal connections of great longevity to the minimal attentions strangers may devote to one another in a fleeting contact. And the consequences of such varied relationships for actual cultural flow have hardly begun to be subjected to scholarly attention.

The second thing is that, in the long run, they can hardly be seen one by one in isolation either, for the point of Marriott and Cohn's argument is surely that they must be viewed in the aggregate, as a pattern of parallel, crosscutting or overlapping connections. Furthermore, between the more symmetrical and the more asymmetrical linkages, as far as the variables of scale and directionality are concerned, one can also discern an interplay; the way individuals draw on the media, for one thing, is hardly independent of their more immediate personal experiences.

A network ethnography of the way people become drawn into a more globalized existence, then, may show how they get involved sequentially in more transnational linkages running in large part parallel to one another. Someone may begin, say, by working for a transnational corporation or acquiring kin abroad. This beginning long-distance link may be of a fairly personal nature, with some rather specific content of meaning. In the process of maintaining it, however, the same individual may get entangled in yet other relationships. He may go abroad to visit his kin or to continue his career and then get involved in a much wider range of new ties, of varied contents, as part of a temporary round of life. As he returns to his point of origin, he may strive to maintain several of these more specific relationships, but he may also seek out other channels for the same kind of more generalized cultural content – developing new media habits, returning as a tourist, cultivating the appropriate expatriate colony in his home country, preferring the company of other locals with similar experiences. The single transnational relationship, in such instances, turns out to have served as a starting point for the build-up of a much more internally varied cluster of transnational links, a broader transnational orientation, a shift in cultural allegiances. And vice versa, that beginning relationship can also be of the more impersonal kind; someone is drawn to a distant place by media representations and acquires personal connections by going there. Either way, there is a cumulative microstructuring of what I would estimate is in the aggregate a fairly sizeable part of the new social landscape of the global ecumene.

It may be illuminating to compare this notion of the distribution and development of parallel network links of varied character with the conceptions of cultural brokerage, mostly at the local/national interface, which developed in anthropology in the 1950s and 1960s.[15] The old-fashioned cultural broker, I believe, was someone who had a fairly well-defined functional connection to the world outside the locality; this connection was well known to others in the locality, and there were not many people of this kind. Moreover, the world outside, to the extent that it was confined to what was structured as a nation, tended to be more or less unicentric. In contrast, what we now seem to see are transnational orientations which, in their sequential development, are both more widespread and probably more random in their distribution within local populations and which, as matters of individual agency in the day-to-day management of meaning, are not so obvious and transparent to others in the local context. Quite possibly, these cultural orientations are also more polycentric, as the combination of personal and impersonal ties may more often orient people in different directions.

CULTURE IN CHAINS

Finally, network ideas may guide us towards a more orderly view of the cultural processes of globalization by pointing to the series of phases which meanings and meaningful forms pass through, and in which they may be consecutively reconstructed, as they move through linked relationships.

We remember, from about a quarter-century ago, Marshall McLuhan's vision of the emergent global village, where through electronic communication everyone would be instantly available to everybody else. This would be a 'retribalized' world, with a technology allowing the simulation of the small-scale. (McLuhan made effective use of anthropological metaphors, although he had mostly contempt for academic anthropologists.) The idea of global reach through a single great leap, too, has been central for those critics of transnational cultural flow through the media who have been more concerned than McLuhan with their strong tendency towards asymmetry – perhaps some few people can reach almost everybody else in one step, but these others cannot really reach back (and this is hardly our idea of a village).

We have already noticed that Marriott (1959), in his interpretation of changing channels of cultural transmission in India, took a similar view of greater distances being covered in fewer moves, with intermediate points being shut out as new technologies of transportation and communication came on the scene. Nonetheless, it seems that in globalization the shorter steps are frequently still there, again often being taken side by side with the great leaps, as it were.

Let me say something about transnational centre-periphery relationships in culture along these lines. Certainly there is a varyingly strong yet unmistakable tendency towards spatial centring at the global level not only in the more asymmetrically organized channels of cultural flow, such as those organized by mass media and transnational cultural markets, but also in what I have delineated as more symmetrically organized networks of one kind or other. The gathering spots, the institutions around which networks cluster, the specialized non-mass media belong in a few major countries and a few world cities more often than they belong anywhere else.

One obvious way of looking at the part played by these centres within the global ecumene is to trace how culture makes its way through network links of different kinds, often parallel to one another, as suggested before, but also ordered serially, towards the periphery. One could see this as a kind of 'trickling down', but what is certainly needed here is a rather muscular sociology of diffusion which attends to the different conditions for the collective management of meaning in each set of relationships – conditions which can presumably result in culture's being renegotiated and reconstructed as well as simply transmitted. In my studies of contemporary Nigerian culture, I have been impressed with the strong centre-periphery orientation which has in large part changed what used to be a mosaic of mostly locally oriented cultures into a national culture ordered by a somewhat ambiguous hierarchy of small, intermediate, and large urban centres headed ultimately not really by Lagos, the national capital, as much as by London and New York (cf. Hannerz 1987). Media, commoditized culture, the education system, and the movement of people all draw this hierarchy together in different constellations of linkages. There is indeed some flow of meaning and meaningful form by a single step from top more or less to bottom, but at each intermediate level there are also those sophisticates with some personal experience of life at least one step nearer the centre. And their impact as local cultural models of metropolitanism is at once personal and invested with understandings which people can draw from other channels. The network continuum I am trying to suggest here is well represented at its end points by two words in twentieth-century Nigerian English: 'beento', the term emerging in the late colonial era for someone who has been to England, or elsewhere overseas, returning with metropolitan cultural capital; and 'bush', the epithet for anything rude and ignorant, not really part of the civilized world.

The tracing of cultural currents from centre to periphery, however, hardly gives us the complete view of the place of centres in the contemporary global ecumene. Elsewhere, taking my point of departure in Redfield and Singer's (1954) paper 'The Cultural Role of Cities', I have recently tried to sketch how today's major world cities perform their cultural role through the local interactions particularly of managerial élites, cultural specialists of many kinds (artists, writers, film-makers, designers, etc.), low-income Third World migrant populations, and tourists, all transnationally mobile (cf. Hannerz n.d.b). These are interactions occurring variously through personal acquaintance, the fleeting relationships of urban public places, and the impersonal relationships in cultural markets of different scope. Again, there are chains of relationships here, perhaps transnational at one end, local in the middle, and transnational again, by way of media or geographical mobility, at the other. By way of such chains, the simple fare of the folk may become, suitably modified, the latest in ethnic cuisine or fast food, and Third World music may become first ethnopop and then world music. The world city is a world city not by being the origin of all things but as much by being a cultural switchboard through which the more or less peripheral cultures can reach one another.

CONCLUSION: THE NETWORK OF NETWORKS

John Barnes (1972: 1), whose Norwegian study was so important in triggering the 1960s and 1970s wave of interest in network analysis, wrote cautiously, as the end of that period was approaching, that perhaps 'network' would turn out to be just another word of very temporary popularity: 'it sounds smart for a few years but like many other trendy terms means all things to all men, and will drop out of use when fashions change'. Whether network concepts at the time of their greatest visibility were applied too broadly or too narrowly for their own good, and ours, may be a matter of argument.[16] I have attempted to argue here, however, that the network remains useful as a root metaphor when we try to think in a reasonably orderly way (without necessarily aiming at rigour of measurement) about some of the heterogeneous sets of often long-distance relationships which organize culture in the world now – in terms of cumulative change or enduring diversity. One may indeed think of the global ecumene as a single large network, and perhaps the chain of even rather personal existing links that it would take to connect any two randomly chosen individuals within it may turn out to be surprisingly short.[17] Yet when I have described the global ecumene as a 'network of networks', this has been to underscore the point that at the same time as network ideas are 'less totalistic, more pluralistic . . . decentralized, mutable' (Marcus 1989: 8), any networks to which we choose to devote special attention do eventually belong within something wider yet.[18]

As a matter of ethnographic research and writing, dealing with the global ecumene in network terms will require of us first of all that we abstain from an *a priori* privileging of local social relationships over those operating over greater distances, and secondly that we endeavour to close whatever gap we may find between the relatively micro- and the relatively macro- by depicting in some instances the asymmetry of scale in certain relationships and in others the aggregation of parallel although sometimes heterogeneous linkages.[19] No doubt there is room for more experimentation here, in the field as well as in the text. And this takes me once more back to Kroeber (1953: 264). Comparing historians with anthropologists, he noted that 'while fundamentally the two groups aim at fairly parallel objectives, anthropologists can be roughly compared to reporters, historians to rewrite men or editors'. Kroeber's point, of course, was that historians work mostly with extant documents, whereas anthropologists produce their own. Yet the difference is also one of overview and organization. As cultural historians of the present, and not least as they aim at portraying in words the global network of networks, social anthropologists may find themselves moving between different scales and integrating their own work more closely with that of others, and so they may have to shift, as producers of text, between being reporters and being editors.

NOTES

1 This paper is written within the 'World System of Culture' project in the Department of Social Anthropology, Stockholm University. Support for the project from the Swedish Research Council for the Humanities and Social Sciences is gratefully acknowledged. Further publications resulting from the project will be referred to below. The general point of view towards network analysis on which I draw here has been developed in Hannerz (1980: 163 ff., 242 ff.).

2 Janet Abu-Lughod, in a comment at the symposium on 'Culture, Globalization, and the World-System', at the State University of New York, Binghamton, April 1, 1989.

3 Cf. Marcus (1986) and Marcus and Fischer (1986: 84 ff.), commenting in particular on Marxism as an available macro-framework; also Hannerz (1989a).

4 It would also seem that 'global ecumene' is rather less suggestive of uniformity than either 'world culture' or 'world civilization' (see Hannerz 1989b).

5 A 'Manchester connection' was clearly important here; among many attempts to review and systematize network anthropology, the better-known were probably those by John Barnes (1968, 1972) and Clyde Mitchell (1969, 1973, 1974).

6 In the sociology of science, too, there has been a strong interest in scholarly and intellectual networks which is relevant to the kind of analysis of cultural organization advocated here.

7 The young Bruce Kapferer (1969) thus stayed in a single room of a mining establishment, with 23 people, for a study often held to have been in some ways exemplary; Jeremy Boissevain (1973), on the other hand, trying to take an inventory of the personal networks of two Maltese schoolteachers, found 638 persons in the one network and 1,751 in the other. See also Barth's (1978: 164) comment.

8 My own first paper drawing on network concepts was indeed on gossip (Hannerz 1967); for further discussion of the characteristics of microcultures see Wulff (1988).

9 I am referring here to the issues involving the nature of cultural transmission raised, for example, by Bloch (1985: 27 ff.).

10 For another exploration of personal networks in relation to culture, see Lithman's (1988) paper on some Muslim immigrants in Sweden in the same volume.

11 The fourth tendency identified there is obviously an extreme instance: solitude.

12 The classic work on cosmopolitans and locals is Merton's (1957: 387 ff.); I have tried to place it in the context of the global ecumene (Hannerz 1990).

13 I am grateful to Marilyn Strathern for drawing my attention to the complementary relationship between my conceptions of cosmopolitanism and creolization.

14 The Wallersteinian version of world-system theory, of course, has tended not to devote much attention to culture at all or to consider it in strictly ideological terms. The more anthropological adaptation which I have primarily in mind here is above all exemplified by Wolf (1982).

15 This interest also seems to have been inspired not least by Redfield (1956); for prominent examples see Wolf (1956) and Geertz (1960).

16 See also a critical review article from the same period by Sanjek (1974: 596):

> if anthropologists view network studies as a special field of inquiry and practitioners encourage this view, we can expect increasingly technical and increasingly trivial results. In view of the pressures in academia to carve out and defend small intellectual niches, there is good reason to fear that this will occur.

17 I have in mind here Milgram's (e.g., 1969) well-known 'small world' experiment, showing how rather randomly chosen individuals within the United States could reach one another in five or six network steps. It may be that the same experiment done on a global scale would show that the number of links would not have to increase much as long as individuals with transnational connections were inserted into the chain at an early point.

18 The 'network of networks' formulation is inspired by Craven and Wellman (1974).

19 See in this connection the comment by two prominent sociological symbolic interactionists (Fine and Kleinman 1983) on the uses of network concepts in addressing macrosociological concerns.

REFERENCES

Barnes, J. A. (1954) 'Class and committees in a Norwegian island parish', *Human Relations* 7: 39–58.

——(1968) 'Networks in political process', in M. J. Swartz (ed.) *Local-level Politics*, Chicago: Aldine.

——(1972) *Social Networks*, Reading, MA: Addison-Wesley.

Barth, F. (1978) 'Scale and network in urban Western society', in F. Barth (ed.) *Scale and Social Organization*, Oslo: Universitetsforlaget.

——(1987) *Cosmologies in the Making*, Cambridge: Cambridge University Press.

——(1989) 'The analysis of culture in complex societies', *Ethnos* 54: 120–42.

Bloch, M. (1985) 'From cognition to ideology', in R. Fardon (ed.) *Power and Knowledge*, Edinburgh: Scottish Academic Press.

Boissevain, J. (1973) 'An exploration of two first-order zones', in J. Boissevain and J. C. Mitchell (eds) *Network Analysis*, The Hague: Mouton.

Bott, E. (1957) *Family and Social Network*, London: Tavistock.

Coser, R. L. (1975) 'The complexity of roles as a seedbed of individual autonomy', in L. A. Coser (ed.) *The Idea of Social Structure*, New York: Harcourt Brace Jovanovich.

Craven, P. and Wellman, B. (1974) 'The network city', in M. P. Effrat (ed.) *The Community*, New York: Free Press.

Fine, G. A. and Kleinman, S. 1983. 'Network and meaning: an interactionist approach to structure', *Symbolic Interaction* 6: 97–110.

Geertz, C. (1960) 'The Javanese Kijaji: the changing role of a cultural broker', *Comparative Studies in Society and History* 2: 228–49.

Gerholm, T. (1988) 'Three European intellectuals as converts to Islam: cultural mediators or social critics?', in T. Gerholm and Y. G. Lithman (eds) *The New Islamic Presence in Western Europe*, London: Mansell.

Goodenough, W. H. (1971) *Culture, Language, and Society*, Reading, MA: Addison-Wesley.

Hamelinck, C. T. (1983) *Cultural Autonomy in Global Communications*, New York: Longman.

Hannerz, U. (1967) 'Gossip, networks, and culture in a black American ghetto', *Ethnos* 32: 35–60.

——(1980) *Exploring the City*, New York: Columbia University Press.

——(1982) 'Delkulturerna och helheten', in U. Hannerz, R. Liljeström, and O. Löfgren (eds) *Kultur och medvetande*, Stockholm: Akademilitteratur.

——(1983) *Över gränser*, Lund: Liber.

——(1986) 'Theory in anthropology: small is beautiful? Anthropological theory and complex cultures', *Comparative Studies in Society and History* 28: 362–7.

——(1987) 'The world in creolisation', *Africa* 57: 546–59.

——(1989a) 'Culture between center and periphery: toward a macro-anthropology', *Ethnos* 54: 200–16.

——(1989b) 'Notes on the global ecumene', *Public Culture* 1, 2: 66–75.

——(1990) 'Cosmopolitans and locals in world culture', *Theory, Culture, and Society* 7, 2 and 3: 237–51.

——(1992) *Cultural Complexity*, New York: Columbia University Press.

——(n.d.a.) 'The cultural shaping of agency', in B. Wittrock (ed.) *Social Theory and Human Agency*, Beverly Hills: Sage. In press.

——(n.d.b.) 'The cultural role of world cities', in A. Cohen and K.

Fukui (eds) *The Age of the City*, Edinburgh: Edinburgh University Press. In press.

Kapferer, B. (1969) 'Norms and the manipulation of relationships in a work context', in J. C. Mitchell (ed.) *Social Networks in Urban Situations*, Manchester: Manchester University Press.

Keesing, R. M. (1987) 'Anthropology as interpretive quest', *Current Anthropology* 28: 161–76.

Kroeber, A. L. (1945) 'The ancient *Oikoumenê* as an historic culture aggregate', *Journal of the Royal Anthropological Institute* 75: 9–20.

——(1953) 'The delimitation of civilizations', *Journal of the History of Ideas* 14: 264–75.

Lithman, Y. G. (1988) 'Social relations and cultural continuities: Muslim immigrants and their social networks', in T. Gerholm and Y. G. Lithman (eds) *The New Islamic Presence in Western Europe*, London: Mansell.

Marcus, G. E. (1986) 'Contemporary problems of ethnography in the modern world system', in J. Clifford and G. E. Marcus (eds) *Writing Culture*, Berkeley: University of California Press.

——(1989) 'Imagining the whole: ethnography's contemporary efforts to situate itself', *Critique of Anthropology* 9, 3: 7–30.

Marcus, G. E. and Fischer, M. M. J. (1986) *Anthropology as Cultural Critique*, Chicago: University of Chicago Press.

Marriott, M. (1959) 'Changing channels of cultural transmission in Indian civilization', in V. Ray (ed.) *Intermediate Societies, Social Mobility, and Communication*, Seattle: American Ethnological Society.

Marriott, M. and Cohn, B. S. (1958) 'Networks and centres in the integration of Indian civilization', *Journal of Social Research* (Ranchi, Bihar) 1: 1–9.

Mattelart, A. (1983) *Transnationals and the Third World*, South Hadley: Bergin and Garvey.

Merton, R. K. (1957) *Social Theory and Social Structure*, rev. and enlgd ed., Glencoe: Free Press.

Milgram, S. (1969) 'Interdisciplinary thinking and the small world problem', in M. Sherif and C. W. Sherif (eds) *Interdisciplinary Relationships in the Social Sciences*, Chicago: Aldine.

Mitchell, J. C. (1969) 'The concept and use of social networks', in J. C. Mitchell (ed.) *Social Networks in Urban Situations*, Manchester: Manchester University Press.

——(1973) 'Networks, norms, and institutions', in J. Boissevain and J. C. Mitchell (eds) *Network Analysis*, The Hague: Mouton.

——(1974) 'Social networks', *Annual Review of Anthropology* 3: 279–99.

Moore, S. F. (1986) *Social Facts and Fabrications*, Cambridge: Cambridge University Press.

Radcliffe-Brown, A. R. (1940) 'On social structure', *Journal of the Royal Anthropological Institute* 70: 1–12.

Redfield, R. (1956) *Peasant Society and Culture*, Chicago: University of Chicago Press.

——(1962) *Human Nature and the Study of Society*, Chicago: University of Chicago Press.

Redfield, R. and Singer, M. (1954) 'The cultural role of cities', *Economic Development and Cultural Change* 3: 53–73.

Sanjek, R. (1974) 'What is network analysis, and what is it good for?', *Reviews in Anthropology* 1: 588–97.

Schiller, H. I. (1976) *Communication and Cultural Domination*, White Plains: M. E. Sharpe.

Schwartz, T. (1978a) 'Where is the culture? Personality and the distributive locus of culture', in G. D. Spindler (ed.) *The Making of Psychological Anthropology*, Berkeley and Los Angeles: University of California Press.

——(1978b) 'The size and shape of a culture', in F. Barth (ed.) *Scale and Social Organization*, Oslo: Universitetsforlaget.

Singer, M. (1972) *When a Great Tradition Modernizes*, London: Pall Mall Press.

——(1976) 'Robert Redfield's development of a social anthropology of civilizations', in J. V. Murra (ed.) *American Anthropology: The Early Years*, St Paul: West.

——(1988) 'Symbolism of the center, the periphery, and the middle', in L. Greenfield and M. Martin (eds) *Center: Ideas and Institutions*, Chicago: University of Chicago Press.

Srinivas, M. N. and Béteille, A. (1964) 'Networks in Indian social structure', *Man* 64: 165–8.

Wallace, A. F. C. (1961) *Culture and Personality*, New York: Random House.

Wolf, E. (1956) 'Aspects of group relations in a complex society: Mexico', *American Anthropologist* 58: 1065–78.

——(1982) *Europe and the People without History*, Berkeley and Los Angeles: University of California Press.

Wulff, Helena. (1988) *Twenty Girls*, Stockholm: Department of Social Anthropology, Stockholm University.

Parts and wholes
The individual and society

Part II

Parts and wholes
The individual and society

Chapter 3

Comparison, a universal for anthropology
From 're-presentation' to the comparison of hierarchies of values

Daniel de Coppet

This paper presents some thoughts on the difficult relationship between modern ideology and the effort to understand the 'social'. It examines the present difficulties of our scientific discipline and proposes that our research should always and deliberately be placed in a comparative perspective.[1]

Social anthropology takes as its 'object' the social dimension, that is, that which members of a particular society (not humankind in general) share in the ensemble of their activities. What they share is that which, 'for all of them', is self-evident. What are we to call such an 'object'? Certainly not simply 'customs', or 'habits', or 'manners'. 'Mentality', 'representations', 'ideology', 'morals', 'values', stress different aspects of the matter, but all bear witness to the richness and importance of the anthropological domain. What is shared appears, on consideration, to have a certain relation with what is not shared and is, for that very reason, of lesser value. We can surely agree that this difference among 'value-ideas' indicates a minimum of order, of 'hierarchy', in the etymological sense that Louis Dumont has reinvented (that is, given new consistency) for social anthropology.

SOCIAL ANTHROPOLOGY IN MODERN SOCIETY

I take as my point of departure something that seems to me an achievement and at the same time presents a major difficulty for our discipline: in the course of its prolonged development, modern ideology, by making the individual (the autonomous subject) the ultimate value (see Dumont 1986 [1983]), has rendered society itself less and less *imaginable*. Ever since the Middle Ages, and most notably since the Enlightenment, society, experienced and understood as a whole, has been gradually but continuously devalued, if not completely obliterated. The conclusion of this slow progression is that society is now considered as a simple collection of individuals, 'a pile of sand': 'Speaking properly, a thing composed of parts is never really *one*. It is *one* only by external denomination, like a pile of sand, or an army' (Leibniz 1987 [1716]: 102, from a letter finished on January 27, 1716, eight and a half months before his death on November 14 of that year, my translation). These metaphors lead us to think that for Leibniz society was, in opposition to an army, 'really *one*'. It was indeed 'by external denomination' that society, reduced to a collection of individuals, slowly began to appear as an object separated and distinguished from the rest of the universe and soon as a sort of container – or, worse, an iron collar – for the multitude of individual, autonomous human destinies. What could be more judicious and exalting, at the end of the nineteenth century, than to make of society, distanced from the ultimate value but still partly experienced, a new object of science, of sociology? What could be more difficult, as well, than to discover it 'from the outside' as an object while at the same time understanding it 'from the inside' as a subject existing independently, organized and coherent – an entity as complex and entire in its permanence as the universe itself?

If the primacy of the individual as ultimate value had left the field clear for the scientific consideration of society, one was nonetheless forced to observe that not all societies had taken the same route, that there existed forms of sociality different from ours, and that even our own evidenced significant synchronic and diachronic variations. During these very rich years at the origin of anthropology and sociology, Tönnies discovered in *Gemeinschaft*, as opposed to *Gesellschaft*, the human dimension par excellence, and Durkheim made of 'society' the first principle, God himself but here on earth.

Since its origins almost a hundred years ago, social anthropology has passed through a long series of enthusiasms: diffusionism, historicism, functionalism, structuralism, ethnoscience and taxonomies, symbolic anthropology, and so forth. Have these various distancings of the object 'society' drawn solely on the register of 'external denominations'? Have they done a bit more, allowing us to perceive a totality which is very much alive, resistant, and often endowed with an astonishingly indissoluble identity? Or have they contributed to blurring even further the 'reality' of societies as such, that is, to reducing to almost nothing what members of each of them share? Judgements on the importance of the results obtained seem to split along a single fault line, evidencing a tension between two opposing attitudes: either the ultimate value accorded the individual is recognized as 'ideological', that is, specific to our society, in which case it takes its place in the sociological enterprise as one (relative) point of view among many; or it is considered universal, not ideological, in which case it is set up as an absolute truth in the search for knowledge of the nature of the social.

We find ourselves face to face here with the conditions peculiar to the anthropo-sociological sciences. That the object 'society' can be distanced reveals the incorporation of the sociological enterprise itself into a society whose own ideology participates in the observation. Those who hold individualism to be truth itself are inclined to believe that they proceed from a self-evident point of view. But this point of view is, to the contrary, socio-logically defined, and, if this fact is not recognized, the object 'society' itself tends to vanish; nothing remains on either side of the act of observation but individuals in interrelation. We thus find ourselves in a situation in which humankind seems to contain only individual totalities. The individualist vision which is at the foundation of anthropo-sociology – insofar as it is taken for absolute truth, as is often the case – thus tends to dismiss one of the fundamental dimensions of humanity, the communal social one. To many contemporary writers, it consequently appears almost presumptuous to attempt to understand a society or, even more crudely, simple-minded to suppose that every society constitutes, in one way or another, a system.

It is true that the dominant modern ideology, by relegating society to an increasingly tenuous existence, ultimately reducing it to a collection of individuals, encourages and partially explains these misgivings of the anthropo-sociological sciences. Is it not tempting for us moderns, who place the ultimate value on the individual, who revere the Rights of Man and defend them as our dearest homeland, and who consider that our predilection is founded in reason and has been crowned by a certain success in the West, in the East, and even in the Far East, to use this ideology and its foundations as tools – held to be superior to all others, even scientifically – for describing societies in general and often, alas, disposing of them to our liking? This last inclination reveals itself clearly in numerous 'development' programs, particularly those to be applied in non-modern societies. Here doubtless is the source of the resounding declarations of certain sociologists and anthropologists for whom society, as a living social being and as a concept, seems a dangerous and purely arbitrary construct which must be dismantled into tiny fragments of experience whose sole agents are individuals. Practices and representations are then held to refer only to individuals in interrelation.

But one must ask oneself, at a more fundamental level, whether being human does not itself imply belonging to a community. Without doubt, the defence of the Rights of Man may lead one to see a danger in a vision of societies as coherent totalities, which in the final analysis may be adjudged oppressive. But is a reverence for the rights of the human person truly incompatible with a judgement that societies also deserve respect? To refuse them such respect means spurning all differences, all specific cultural identities. What is worse, the refusal to take into account this communal social dimension inherent in the human condition, far from offering protection against totalitarian deviations, may lead to them. The intention to recognize only individuals often assumes the character of a destructive mania.

On the contrary, a sense of belonging to humanity as a whole and of slowly constructing the bases of a planetary society often draws greater impetus and force from a prior affirmation of specific local identities which, once consolidated, become supports for the emergence of a supplementary identity on a larger scale. In our collegial experience as anthropologists, we can see that the recent creation of this European Association is not the consequence of abolishing the differences among our scientific traditions but rather results from a deliberate commitment of each of us to become better acquainted with all of them and to make a greater effort to compare them. We should not, thus, delude ourselves into thinking that comparative sociology, itself an effort to marry the individualist ideal with the existence of the communal social dimension, entails any threat to the universalist point of view of the individual, the foundation – as we recognize – of modern uniqueness and of all scientific effort.

SLIPPAGES OF MEANING

The recent incorporation into anthropology of these extreme tendencies of modern individualist ideology has been accompanied in contemporary Western languages by increasing difficulty in expressing what a society is. It is indeed in the nature of things that certain words, as they gradually cease to be bearers of the ultimate value, so completely lose their original meanings that new words must be found to bear those meanings. For example, the word 'universitas' in the thirteenth century meant a 'community considered as a totality'. Its holist tenor was thereafter lost, and it was replaced by the word 'society', understood, however, only as simple association or companionship (cf. Onions 1986 [1916]: 256 § 'society' in the work of Shakespeare). This led at the end of the nineteenth century to the revival by Tönnies of the pairs *Gemeinschaft/Gesellschaft* and *Naturwille/Kürwille*.

The attempt to understand human societies collides with the fact that, concurrently with the modification of what is shared and what is felt as self-evident, our language itself has followed in the wake of modern ideology. Language tends thus imperceptibly to obliterate the traces of its own evolution, rendering it extremely difficult to identify the slippages of meaning which have occurred. We must then make an effort to register, along this continuum of slippages, certain leaps of meaning whose height and direction may be measured.

If we follow Richard Rorty when he sets forth for us 'the story of the domination of the mind of the West by ocular metaphors, within a social perspective' (1980: 13), we may well raise the question whether such ocular metaphors are adequate not for coming to know 'the world' (which is not our province) but rather for understanding societies – for discovering what is shared by the members of a community. Can one indeed understand the social relations and the various ideologies of specific societies when the seeing subject is increasingly distanced from the object seen? The answer to this question is not at all simple. Distancing a society different from one's own indeed supposes that one has succeeded in relativizing one's own, which thus enters into the act of observation only as a point of view. But this cross-observation, which as 'cross' is necessarily comparative, must then be founded upon active participation in the other society, considered from within as 'self-evident', as well. Of the very numerous consequences of this ocular distancing of the object, one is the separation of consciousness from experience, another the assertion that consciousness controls all activities. In anthropology, this demand is shocking, since consciousness of what is shared by others can only exist through what is shared by us.

Likewise, the constant and increasing modern tendency to 'separate' widens the rift between practices and representations, and this led anthropology at one point to raise the question whether representations should even be considered fundamental social facts. Apart from the positive response of structural anthropology, which maintained that they were complementary, two other sorts of answers were forthcoming, depending on whether priority was attributed to practices or to representations. This elevated the initial separation into a sort of conflict between 'realists' and 'idealists', between 'political' and 'symbolic' anthropologists. Nonetheless, we now all agree that this opposition finds its limits in the fact that, far from characterizing a difference between societies, it was applied directly, as if these opposing tendencies of modern ideology were adequate tools for the description of societies.

WHICH REPRESENTATION?

Among these ocular metaphors, the various acceptations in French and English of the words 'represent' and 'representation' are rich in surprises for our contemporary understanding, all the more so since they have been the object of critical analyses by the phenomenologists and then by Wittgenstein, Heidegger, and numerous others. In English, since the fourteenth century, 'to represent' has meant

> making present: in the physical sense of representing oneself or another . . . but also in the sense of making present in the mind . . . and to the eye, in painting . . . or in plays. . . . But a crucial extension also occurred in C14 when *represent* was used in the sense of 'symbolise' or 'stand for'. . . . It is clear that at this stage there was considerable overlap between the sense (a) of making present to the mind and the sense (b) of standing for something that is not present. What was eventually a divergence between these senses, in some uses, might not at first have been perceived as a divergence at all.
>
> (Williams 1976: 222–3)

The contrast is accentuated between an efficacious activity and a simple equivalence.

In French, the word *représentation* does not always suggest images which stand for something else but may also refer to actions which 'make present anew'. (The German word *Vorstellung*, literally 'presentation', does not imply this idea of 'reappearance' which is so important in both English and French.) In an earlier French, a *représentation* was a wooden structure which had the virtue of 'making present *anew*', especially at funeral services. This structure *repeated a presence which at the same time became fundamentally new, that is, efficacious and creative*. What sort of innovation is involved here?

In his book *The Royal Funeral Ceremony in Renaissance France* (1987), the historian Ralph Giesey, a disciple of Kantorowicz, describes an interesting error of interpretation of the word *représentation* which puts us on the right track. The confusion arose from the fact that a seventeenth-century scholar, in his translation of the Latin chronicle of Saint-Denis recounting the funeral ceremonies of Bertrand du Guesclin in 1389, had referred to 'the *représentation* of the illustrious deceased', which later readers took to be the deceased's effigy. The Latin original, finally published in 1836, spoke clearly, however, of 'a funeral litter covered by a silken pall' and not of an effigy. Giesey was able to establish that the translation by *représentation* was well founded when he discovered the following definition of *représentation* in Littré's *Dictionnaire de la langue française*: "'a kind of empty coffin, on which a pall is laid for a religious ceremony". And Littré adds: "In the Middle Ages, a cast, painted figure which, in funeral rites, represented the deceased"' (Giesey 1987: 137, my translation). We see how, on the one hand, something (which remains to be specified) is 'made present *anew*' in the form of an empty coffin and, on the other, an effigy of the deceased replaces the deceased himself. In the first acceptation, the empty coffin makes newly present the deceased's disappearance, while in the second, the effigy 'stands for' the deceased – which is, on consideration, really quite a different matter. Thus the act of making newly present the disappearance of a human being by means of an empty coffin has been eclipsed by the presentation of a 'living image' of the deceased. And this is the very path followed in French by the word *représentation* and the one it took in English, which led the verb 'to represent' from the sense 'to place before the eyes' to the totally different senses of 'to put in the place of' or 'to signify by an image'.

This slippage of meaning invites the question of the quality of the presence repeated and obtained by this *re-présentation*. But first, what does the 'representation' consist of? Essentially of two objects, one superimposed on the other: an empty coffin or even a simple wooden 'funeral litter' and, covering it, a pall, often heavily embroidered, called a *poile*. We thus have a space circumscribed horizontally by the contours of a litter or a coffin and marked vertically by a separation between what is above and what is below the *poile*. The most significant object here is the *poile* itself, which establishes a division and structures the entirety of the 'representation'. The meaning of this separation may better be grasped if we know that it appears in an impressive series of rites. Furetière's *Dictionnaire universel* of 1690 (my translation) indicates that the *poile* is a

> portable baldachin supported by columns, and composed of a canopy [*un ciel*, also 'sky, firmament, heavens'] and valances, under which the Blessed Sacrament is placed when it is carried through the streets. It is also carried above the heads of Kings and Prelates in their entries and other ceremonies, in order to honor them. . . . The *poile* is usually made of embroidered velvet.
>
> *Poile* is the name given to a pall placed over a coffin during the ceremony of a funeral cortège and a burial. *Poiles* are made of black velvet. . . . The same name is given to the cloth held above those who marry.

The *poile* thus separates two regions of the cosmos: what is above, which is celestial and in the strict sense divine, and what is below, which is not but which, through this covering composed of a 'canopy' and 'valances', is hallowed by the divine. Thus under the *poile*, embroidered with flowers, crosses, or stars, one could see going by the Blessed Sacrament, kings, prelates, and couples on their wedding days. In the *Sacramentary* of the bishop Warmundus of Ivrea, dating from the beginning of the eleventh century, a body on its way to the church and thence to the cemetery is depicted covered by a *poile* decorated with small cruciform flowers (cf. Schmitt 1990: 216–21). The *poile* covering the Ivrea funeral litter marks the separation between the world here below and the Kingdom of Heaven.

In the case of the 'representation' composed of an empty coffin or an empty funeral litter, what is made present anew is not the deceased, as our modern conceptions, attached to the idea of separate identities, might mislead us to believe, but the overall configuration composed of two opposed worlds – the earthly world from which the deceased has departed and the Kingdom of Heaven which he is to enter. It is the presentation not just of an absent body but of the universe in its totality and its mystery. Mystery is 'that by which the thing works its effects through the sign and by which the sign participates in the efficacy of the thing' (de Lubac 1949: 63). This 'representation' is a ritual act which, through the divine promise of the resurrection, hallows the deceased in his journey from this world to the next. This mystery and this journey, as well as the repetition of this 'absence here below/presence in the next world', recall and re-present a fundamental disappearance, that of Christ's body from the Holy Sepulchre on the way to his resurrection. Giesey calls our attention to this resemblance and notes:

> The possibility of a direct link between the 'procession' of royal funerals, during which an effigy was carried under a canopy, and the procession of Corpus Christi, where the host is similarly treated, is suggested to us by the fact that a parallel between these two processions is drawn at least twice in the fifteenth-century chronicles.
>
> (Giesey 1987: 286 n. 49, my translation)

Giesey goes on: 'Another ceremony seems much closer to me, that of Christ's Sepulchre at Easter, when a host or a cross, or even a representation of Christ, placed under a baldachin, was carried to a tomb'. Thus the funeral rite repeats for the deceased – royal or not – Christ's disappearance from this tomb, one of the fundamental events of Christianity. The empty coffin or empty litter, as a *re-présentation*, at once recaptures a prior experience – death to earthly life – and constructs a new experience – birth into eternal life – around the threshold depicted by the *poile*.

But we must be careful here to see the enormous contrast between the empty coffin, which calls us on to eternal life, and the presentation of the royal effigy, which, despite the king's death, conserves intact the crown's powers here below until the enthronement of his successor. During this 'ceremonial interregnum which

existed between a king's death and the coronation of the following one – a vacuum that the funeral ceremony contributed
to filling' (Giesey 1987: 286, my translation) – the former king
was considered still alive. The effigy 'stood for' the living king,
his *dignitas* intact, over whom the canopy of the *poile* extended.
If we consider carefully these two 'representations', we see that
a gap has appeared between a ritual act, part of the mystery of
the universe which this action itself confirms by its opening on
to eternal life, and a simple substitute for the living king which
conserves intact the royal principle.

In the former case, a ritual act reconstitutes and confirms the
order of the universe: it is a form of totalization. In the latter,
there is a copying of the thing and the beginning of a separation,
within the earthly domain, between the body of the king and
the *dignitas* of the kingdom, between the king's 'true body' and
his 'mystical' or 'political' body (cf. Kantorowicz 1957; Giesey
1960; 1987; Marin 1981), between the thing and its sign. We can
understand the enormous difference between a ritual act, which
is a sort of repetition and as such *creative*, in harmony with the
mystery, and a substitution, which is a device of the political
domain in the earthly world and a dramatic artifice distancing the
literal from the figurative, fact from idea, what is real from what
is thought. The unity of the mystery of Christ-as-totality has been
succeeded by a reference to the 'body' as a general, universal form.
The 'mystical' and thereafter 'political' body of the king becomes
analogous to the flesh-and-blood body and to the body of human
societies and gradually loses its relationship with the totality. A
veritas corporis has been substituted for the truth and reality of
the mystery as totality and imposed as the sole reference (de Lubac
1949), rationally opposing the identical to the analogous, the latter
being conceived of as a sort of shimmering attenuation of the real.
Since the reference has been completely transformed, in order to
vest the earthly world with ultimate value, the 'representation'
effigy no longer has anything to say about the mystery that the
'representation' funeral litter accomplished in passing from one
side of the *poile* to the other, from below to above.

Closer to us, in modern French, Littré indicates that the word
présence has a liturgical meaning: 'in a church, [the] technical name
of the wooden structure simulating the presence of the coffin, and
used in services for the dead'. With this *présence*, which makes
reference only to the coffin, we are several centuries away from

the mystery recognized in Christ-as-totality (at once man in the world and God).

REPRESENTATION IN ANTHROPOLOGY

Thus the word *représentation* – the *poile* laid on an empty litter – which, by recalling the exemplary resurrection of Christ and pointing the way to the Kingdom of Heaven, renewed the fundamental order, became a simple effigy, a sort of 'image'-pole of a double opposition – to the 'real' on the one hand, to any form of ritual action on the other. Representation is understood, then, as an 'image', held to be free and in rather loose association both with facts (as a copy or simulacrum) and with actions (as theatre or fiction). In this devalued sense, representation is nowadays often considered a sign of absence and of death and sometimes assumes the aspect of a funeral procession, a frozen order, a closed system, an abstraction. Following from this, one might say that only individual actions become presence: distinct from reflection, they belong to the real, the living, the spontaneous, the not-thought.

On the contrary, the representation composed of the empty coffin or funeral litter partakes of the mystery of Christ-as-totality. It clarifies, in the most sober fashion, the essence of Christian humanism. We can understand as well that this sense of *représentation* may correspond to 'image' in the Christian configuration of values. On this question, the definitive references are to be found in the texts of Saint Bernard de Clairvaux, for whom man is to be judged entirely in accordance with his greater or lesser likeness (*similitudo*) to God. Image, for him, is thus a tension impelling us toward the Word of God, which is absolute Image. This Image is 'justice of justice, wisdom of wisdom, truth of truth, just as it is light of the light of God. The soul, which is not image, is nothing of all that, but is capable and desirous of it, and that is doubtless what is meant by "created in His image"' (1953: 816, my translation).

Of the two acceptations of *représentation*, we can see that the first (the empty litter covered by the *poile*) has its place, 'in the image of God', above the *poile*, while the second (the effigy), 'in the image of the living body', is situated here below. In this second case, the ultimate value has come to be vested entirely in the earthly world; all tension is located beneath the *poile*, in relation to earthly goals, and linked to the *veritas corporis*. We know that, by the time of the funeral of Francis the First, the effigy was no longer laid on the coffin in the funeral procession and that the *poile* was carried not above his effigy but behind it. The unity of the mystery was dismissed in favor of rational distinctions which can be observed in the ordering of the funeral procession: first the king's dead body in its coffin covered with a black *poile*, then the king's effigy adorned with red and golden garments, and just behind it another *poile* or baldachin, heavily embroidered. The sober and total *représentation* was replaced by a depiction of the earthly world with, in addition to the black *poile*, the rich colours once restricted to the heavenly kingdom.

This gradual transformation of the meaning of the word 'representation' perhaps also allows us better to grasp the progressive separation between subject and object and the distancing of action from thought, fact from value. All these developments may be understood as stages in the consolidation of individualist ideology; value is no longer vested in facts, held to be objective, or in thought, held to be free, but only in the self-explanatory actions of individuals.

The creative fusion among activity, thought, and reality thus gave way to a dissolution which distanced the object from the individual subject. The panoply of different ocular metaphors led to the generalized conquest of the object by the subject, with the appearance of various 'world views' or *Weltanschauungen* which were all diverse ways of taking possession of the world. The omnipotence of the subject also had a necessary complement: soon nothing at all remained beyond the subject, which asserted itself as not only victorious but autonomous, its own system, with the system of what remained of the rest of the world converted into object. This isolation of the individual subject within its self-reference separated it at once from the cosmos, from nature, and from the communal social dimension.

Once this solitary universality of the human subject is posited, what are we to do with other societies and cultures? Two options seem to present themselves: (1) to reduce the otherness of the social dimension to the otherness of autonomous individual subjects 'inventing among themselves' a single, unstable culture defined as the resultant of a swarm of actions of individuals (this individual self-reference could be described as a sort of nihilism and the amputation of any communal social relationship); or (2) to 'relativize' the notion of truth, considering it to have meaning only in the context of a particular social ideology, with the inevitable consequence that societies and their 'world views' become radically incommensurable. In either event, the universalist ambitions of science appear bankrupt. The way is left clear for the 'raw facts', for conflict, for the dominance of relations of force – strangely enough, the only 'system' recognized as exemplary of nature.

In light of the contrast, which I have attempted to clarify, between the two 'representations' witnessed in the funeral ceremonies of the Middle Ages and the Renaissance, one can understand the interest of the phenomenological perspective, which, by insisting on intentionality, attempts to restore to knowledge the virtues of an action constitutive of phenomena. Unfortunately, the intentionality in question refers back to the individual consciousness, a point of view founded on our society's exclusive preference for projections of an omnipotent subjectivity.

Heidegger (1962 [1949]) certainly goes farther in his critique of the concept of 'representation'; he considers it constitutive of the old 'metaphysics of subjectivity' whose limits he discerns. Is he not thus in search of another *difference* which would allow us to advance a step farther towards enlightenment? Can Heidegger's deconstruction of metaphysics help us rediscover a certain unity in what science, founded on this particular metaphysics, has ceaselessly separated? Does it begin to open a path on which nature and humankind may find each other once again (see Heidegger's 'epoch of world views' and also Ladrière 1972)?

In social anthropology, it has indeed often proven more a hindrance than a help to maintain the classic separation between subject and object, the opposition of thought to action and of saying to doing, the separation between idea and value, and an understanding of value as 'exiled from the domain of facts' to use Dumont's language (1986 [1983]: 215). Does this observation not set the limits of 'representation-substitution' as the image of so-called universal reality? Does it not lead us to rediscover, in our research itself, the other sense of 'representation', 'to make present anew' – a creative social act which becomes confirmed knowledge and at the same time constitutes a value-fact encompassed by a particular social whole: a society?

It is also remarkable that the difference between what in fact happens in a system (a society) and what is attributed value and shared in that system cannot be expressed unless this difference is compared with a difference of the same sort (between what happens and what is attributed value) in another system (society).

Does this not mean that we must attempt to introduce on each occasion an *active difference* between two distinct value-levels of each system – a difference which is *active* in the sense that it only appears as a result of an interchange between two different perspectives, those of two systems (societies). This sort of active, complex difference constitutes the universal of social anthropology, a relational universal. Communal (and without doubt individual) systems (or identities) may only be comprehended through the relations between systems (societies). Such cross-representation is efficacious in the sense that it 'makes present anew', through mutual understanding, a place where relational truth can manifest itself, in social anthropology. The result is the active comparison of two 'hierarchies of value', the only 'facts' (or value-facts) which are commensurable in social anthropology.

THE CONDITIONS FOR AGREEMENT IN CONTEMPORARY ANTHROPOLOGY

Having posited the preceding, I should also immediately acknowledge that this anthropology of 'hierarchies of value', initiated by Dumont, derives in a sense from the same impulse which has driven certain of our colleagues in anthropology towards relativism and led others to return to an idea of society understood as 'association' (*societas* and not *universitas*), for which they employ the word 'sociality'. We are indeed doubtless all in agreement on the damage done to the social sciences by the excessive atomization of its levels of analysis and by the too rigid separation of subject and object. We are all sensitive to the simplifications imported into anthropology from an outdated ideology of the exact sciences, such as 'mirror' representation, frozen classifications, and the distinction between infra- and superstructure. We are all concerned about the impossible 'reality' of systems of thought severed from action. We also share a recognition that the only truth is relational.

Disagreement persists, however, on the conclusions to be drawn, on the paths which could lead to placing in perspective a universal in anthropology. But why curtail to such a degree the original ambitions of the founders of our discipline? Is it the grandiosity of certain structuralist propositions, sometimes put forward in overly ambitious works offensive to a more modest, research-oriented point of view, which leads us to despair of the conditions of anthropology? Can the serious acceptance of the relativity of social systems make us doubt the urgency of re-presenting anthropologically the modern world and its specific totalitarian demons?

Among these demons as yet quite untamed should we not number an exclusive fascination with the autonomous, living, 'cosmic'[2] individual, a rejection of the relational truth of communal systems, a refusal to take into consideration the hierarchy of values of each system (society)? We can further perceive that, when we attempt to compare individual intentions feature by feature, term by term, there immediately arise contradiction, opposition, conflict, and always on the same unified one-level stage. On the contrary, the consideration of wholes situated beyond the individual, that is, of hierarchies of value traced out by societies, leads anthropology into a surprising, living sphere: that of the cross-representation of an *active difference* between two systems which are incomparable feature by feature but whose respective totalities are nonetheless comparable.[3] Here we encounter a relational universal as it really resounds between human communities.

NOTES

1 Stephen Suffern kindly translated the French version of this paper.
2 In modern ideology, the living individual's incorporation into the cosmos is accepted much more easily than his belonging to a social system. On the contrary, many non-modern societies experience a profound 'socio-cosmic' unity, intermingling cosmos with society.
3 In addition to the references already cited, the following works are relevant: Barraud *et al.* (1984), Boureau (1988), Certeau (1982), Coppet (1990), *Critique* (1985), Dumont (1980 [1966]; 1990), Gilson (1947; 1986), and Tambiah (1985).

REFERENCES

Austin, John Langshaw (1962) *How to Do Things with Words*, Oxford: Oxford University Press.
Barraud, C., Coppet, D. de, Iteanu, A., and Jamous, R. (1984) 'Des relations et des morts, analyse de quatre sociétés vues sous l'angle des échanges', in J. C. Galey (ed.) *Différences valeurs, hiérarchie: Textes offerts à Louis Dumont*, Paris: EHESS.
Bernard, Saint (1953) *Oeuvres mystiques*, Paris: Editions du Seuil.
Boureau, Alain (1988) *Le simple corps du roi: L'impossible sacralité des souverains français, XVe–XVIIe siècle*, Paris: Editions de Paris.
Certeau, Michel de (1982) *La fable mystique XVIe–XVIIe siècle*, Paris: Gallimard.

Coppet, Daniel de (1990) 'The society as an ultimate value and the socio-cosmic configuration', *Ethnos* 1990 (3–4): 140–50.

Critique: La traversée de l'Atlantique (1985) No. 456.

Dumont, Louis (1980 [1966]) *Homo Hierarchicus: The Caste System and Its Implications*, Chicago: University of Chicago Press.

——(1986 [1983]) *Essays on Individualism: Modern Ideology in Anthropological Perspective*, Chicago: University of Chicago Press.

——(1990) 'Sur l'idéologie politique française: Une perspective comparative', *Le Débat*, no. 58.

Giesey, Ralph E. (1960) *The Royal Funeral Ceremony in Renaissance France*, Geneva.

——(1987) *Cérémonial et puissance souveraine, France, XVe–XVIe siècles*, Paris: Armand Colin.

Gilson, Etienne (1947) *La théologie mystique de Saint Bernard*, Paris: Vrin.

——(1986) *La philosophie au Moyen Age*, second ed. rev. and aug., Paris: Payot.

Heidegger, Martin (1962 [1949]) *Chemins qui ne mènent nulle part*, Paris: Gallimard.

Kantorowicz, Ernst H. (1957) *The King's Two Bodies: A Study of Medieval Political Theology*, Princeton: Princeton University Press.

Ladrière, Jacques (1972) 'Représentation et connaissance', in *Encyclopaedia Universalis*.

Leibniz, G. W. (1987 [1716]) 'Lettre à M. de Rémond', in *Discours sur la théologie naturelle des Chinois: Plus quelques écrits sur la question religieuse de Chine*, Paris: L'Herne.

Lubac, Henri de (1949) *Corpus mysticum: L'eucharistie et l'eglise au Moyen Age*, Paris: Aubier Montaigne.

Marin, Louis (1981) *Le portrait du roi*, Paris: Editions de Minuit.

Onions, Charles Talbut (1986 [1919]) *A Shakespeare Glossary*, enl. and rev. Robert D. Eagleson, Oxford: Oxford University Press.

Rorty, Richard (1980) *Philosophy and the Mirror of Nature*, Oxford: Blackwell.

Schmitt, Jean-Claude (1990) *La raison des gestes dans l'Occident médiéval*, Paris: Gallimard.

Tambiah, Stanley Jeyaraja (1985) *Culture, Thought, and Social Action*, Cambridge, Mass., and London: Harvard University Press.

Williams, Raymond (1976) *Keywords: A Vocabulary of Culture and Society*, Glasgow: Fontana.

Chapter 4

Parts and wholes
Refiguring relationships in a post-plural world

Marilyn Strathern

'Parts and wholes' alludes to an intellectual tradition within anthropology in which I can claim no part, though it is part of the wider world in which I live. The reason is unremarkable. Whether that world is conceptualized as British or European or Western, no one person can reproduce it in its entirety. Conversely, one cannot undo the particular processes by which one is reproduced. Or so we – whether we claim to be British or European or Western in our thinking – hold.

De Coppet (1985: 78) has put forward a powerful plea for the study of societies as totalities:

> Comparison is only possible if we analyse the various ways in which societies order their ultimate values. In doing so, we attempt to understand each society as a *whole*, and not as an object dismantled by our own categories.[1]

The task is to compare not subsystems but 'societies in their own right', a holistic vision apt for 'holistic societies', for the problem, he suggests, lies in the interference of the categories that, by contrast, reproduce 'our own individualistic society'.

If I endorse de Coppet's observation, it is to remark that conceptualization is inevitably reconceptualization. The society we think up for the 'Are 'Are, Melanesians from the Solomon Islands, is a transformation of the society we think up for ourselves. For instance, de Coppet says of the 'Are 'Are that far from their society's imparting its own character of permanence to the individuals who compose it, it builds up its character (of permanence) through repeated dissolution into 'the ritual and exchange process of the main elements composing each individual' (1981: 176). Instead of dismantling holistic systems through inappropriate analytical categories, then, perhaps we should strive for a holistic apprehension of the manner in which our subjects dismantle their own constructs. At least as far as Melanesia is concerned, the constructs thereby dismantled or dissolved include life-forms: persons, bodies, and the reproductive process itself.

Contemporary Melanesian ethnography, especially but not only from the Austronesian-speaking seaboard, is developing its own microvocabulary of dissolution. It describes the processes by which the elements that compose persons are dismantled so that the relationships persons carry can be invested anew. This may include both the relations created during life and the procreative (conjugal) relations that created them. A North Mekeo is 'de-conceived' first at marriage and then finally at death (Mosko 1985); Muyuw on Woodlark Island 'end' a parent's marriage when the child dies (Damon 1989); Barok mortuary feasts 'obviate' previous relationships in finally killing the dead (Wagner 1986), a process that for the Sabarl is a 'disassembling' (Battaglia 1990) and on Gawa a 'severance' or 'dissolution' of social ties (Munn 1986). These recall Bloch's (1986) arresting account from elsewhere in the Austronesian-speaking world of the literal 'regrouping' of the dead in their tombs. But if relationships reproductive of persons have to be dissolved at death, other Melanesians see birth as the principal substitutive act by which new relations displace previous ones (Gillison 1991). Indeed, all knowledge of a revelatory kind may appear as decomposition (Strathern 1988a).

These counter-images to the received anthropological metaphors of structure and system have a late-twentieth-century ring to them. However, as Battaglia notes (1990: 218 n. 49), it is important to distinguish post-modernism as 'a movement with roots in the specifically historical problem of the alienating and fragmenting effects of Western socioeconomic and political influences on other cultures' from analytical perspectives (hermeneutic, deconstructivist) that have as their goal 'respect for indigenous ways of conceiving the cultural reproduction of knowledge that are themselves "perspectivist"'. Indeed, one should be as cautious as one is creative with the resonances between cultural fragmentation perceived in the world at large, specific analytical tactics such as deconstruction, and the discovery of relationships being indigenously conceptualized through images of dissolution.

The irony is that what clouds the anthropologists' holistic enterprise in the late twentieth century is no longer individualism. The 'death of the individual' has seen to that. Rather, the problem is the Western dismantling of the very category that once carried the concept of a holistic entity, that is, 'society'. Society was a vehicle for a kind of Western holism, a totalizing concept through which modern people could think the holisms of others. Nowadays it seems to belong more to text than to life.[2] The modernist vision was also a pluralist one, and the pluralist vision of a world full of distinctive, total societies has dissolved into a post-plural one. This is Hannerz's (1988; 1990) cosmopolitanism or creolization, the fragmentary or hybrid global village. Yet it will no more do to shift into the vocabulary of fragmentation because of Western awareness of transnational parochialism than it was ever appropriate to export awareness of nation-states or possessive individuals. At the same time, Battaglia argues (1990: 4), the new vocabulary may well capture indigenous conceptualizations that proved refractory to pluralist models.

The image of hybrid form was in fact already there in the pluralist world. It was not just the replication of like units (a multitude of distinctive but analogous societies) that pluralized anthropological vision, along with others; an equally powerful source of pluralism lay in the way different domains or orders of knowledge were brought together. Here a multitude of perspectives could pluralize the character of anything held up to study. And it is here that we find antecedents for present ideas about fragmenting parts and vanishing wholes.

This chapter is a late-twentieth-century attempt to refigure certain relationships as they have been conceptualized in this recent, pluralist past.[3] The relationships in question belong to an apparently small domain of anthropological inquiry, those Melanesian kinship systems known as cognatic. This is because of the assumption that, despite the insignificance of kinship in Western or Euro-American society, Euro-American systems are similarly cognatic in character. Yet we cannot have it both ways; either both mode of reckoning and degree of significance are comparable or neither is. I suggest that failure to attend to the particularity of our 'own' kinship thinking has also been failure to attend to symbolic processes in anthropological thinking. It is these that have, over the last century or so, both endorsed the concept of society and dissolved it before our eyes.

THE VANISHING OF GARIA SOCIETY

I start with the rebirth of a modernist paradigm. The midcentury in British social anthropology saw, in Kuper's phrase, a phoenix arise from the ashes. In a reconceptualized form segmentary lineage systems, as he observes (1988: 204), turned up everywhere. Among other things, they afforded a powerful equation between societies and groups.

When Lawrence finally published his account of the Garia, he rather daringly had Fortes write the foreword. It was all very well for Fortes to say that eventually the Garia concept of 'thinking on' kinsmen inspired his formulation of kinship amity. The truth is that, in 1950, Lawrence's description of these Melanesians had been a scandal. Looking back, Fortes set out the problem:

> When, fresh from the field, Peter Lawrence enthusiastically described Garia social organization to me, my initial reaction was, shall we say, cautious. What later came to be designated the African segmentary descent group model was still a novelty and to many of us full of promise. Melanesia meant, above all, the Trobriands, Dobu, Manus, the Solomon Islands, and descent groups resembling those of the African Model seemed to occur in all of them. The Garia were conspicuously different. . . . [T]hey seemed to have a structure without boundaries: no genealogical boundaries marking off one group of people from another . . . no local boundaries fixing village sites . . . no political boundaries with neighbouring peoples, no closed ritual associations or exclusive access to economic resources – a society based, in short, not on unilineal descent groups but on ramifying cognatic kinship relations. . . . [T]his fluidity of structure posed the problem of how any sort of social continuity or cohesion could be maintained.

> (Fortes 1984: ix)

The only visible basis for social relations appeared to lie in the way the individual was conceived to be at the centre of radiating ties that formed a security circle:

> The essence of their social organization . . . is the right of the individual to align himself . . . freely with kin on the side of either of his parents. . . . This gives rise to the main problem that, as Radcliffe-Brown . . . points out, confronts all such systems of social organization: how to counteract – how to put boundaries to – the outward extension of kinship ties to farther and farther zones of cousinship.
>
> (Fortes 1984: x)

Garia social organization was there, but where was Garia society?

Drawing on a cognatic terminology, Lawrence eventually produced a model of rights and membership. Garialand was divided into overlapping domains associated with bush gods to whom sets of persons were attached; some 200 named cognatic stocks were scattered through the domains of these gods. Each stock was presumed descended from a sibling set, internally divided between those who traced descent through males and those who traced descent through females (1984: 45). Because of certain male privileges, Lawrence also discerned patrilineages (p. 43). He then drew on another set of Garia terms to describe an individual person's kindred. These were simply indigenous words for the closeness and distance between relatives that made a person the centre of circles of proximity. Close cognates shaded off into distant cognates, each degree of relationship including both matrikin and patrikin.

Lawrence was battling against the then-prevailing cartographic images of social structure that insisted on a boundedness to the division of social interests. The concept of cognatic kinship made it appear as though it were the overlapping demands of kin alignments that created divisions. Social order was thereby apprehended as a plurality of external interests; cohesion was to be found in the security circle, where the kindred could at least be diagrammed (1984: figs 7, 9). Yet the significance of these relationships to a person was stated in a disconcertingly casual manner: 'They are merely those individuals . . . with whom he has safe relationships' (1971: 76).

The problems that Garia posed in 1950 were twofold: first, how to conceptualize a society that was not composed of groups, and second, the relationship of parts to wholes. If groups were the vehicles through which societies presented themselves to their members, then without group membership what was a person a part of?

The problem (for British anthropology) had been posed by Radcliffe-Brown: 'it is only a unilineal system that will permit the division of a society into separate organized kin-groups' (1950: 82).[4] Larger kin groups such as clans 'consisted of' smaller ones such as lineages (1952: 70), and lineages were composed of 'persons' such that 'the principle of the unity of the lineage group' provided a relation which linked 'a given person and all the members of the lineage group' (p. 87). Persons could also be seen as linked in a network of kin relations that constituted 'part of that total network of social relations that I call social structure' (p. 53). With the demonstration of structure came the assertion that between 'various features of a particular kinship system, there is a complex relation of interdependence' such that one may conceptualize 'a complex unity, an organised whole' (p. 53). Radcliffe-Brown could thus call for the comparison of whole systems elucidated by different kinship structures such as those manifest in lineage groups. The whole was known by its internal coherence, and thus its closure.

System, structure, group: these terms are not identical, and are not identical with society, but as a set of comprehensive organizational categories each provided a perspective from which that whole entity could be imagined. The recognition of groups 'by society' was further visualized in the notion that individual persons became part of society by becoming a part of a group. Descent-group theory literally focused on the mediating role of lineages and other corporate constructs in effecting social adulthood, adulthood being equated with membership. In one flight of fancy, Fortes imagined this process in the manner of a child growing from infant to adult status. The maturation of the individual is of paramount concern to society at large, he argued. Thus the domestic group, 'having bred, reared and educated the child,' then 'hands over the finished product to the total society' (1958: 10). As a pre-existing whole, society makes individuals into parts of itself by severing them from other pre-existing domains. Thus 'the whole society' sets itself against 'the private culture of each domestic group' (p. 12).

If individual persons were in this midcentury view made into members of groups/society as a whole, they were also regarded as having naturally pre-existing identities. These derived both from their biological or psychological makeup and from the domestic domain. Since domestic and politico-jural domains were conceptualized as cutting up social life into components that were not reducible to one another, each gave a different perspective on social life; and while they combined in single persons ('Every member of a society is simultaneously a person in the domestic domain and in the politico-jural domain' [Fortes 1958: 12]) they represented quite distinct relational fields. Society appeared simultaneously exclusive of and inclusive of the domestic domain. What made a person a member of society by virtue of his or her politico-jural relations was not what made him or her a member of the domestic group that supplied 'the new recruit'. In short, what gave the part ('the individual') distinctiveness as a whole person was not what made the person a part of the whole society.

The Garia problem can be rephrased: by contrast with what made a Garia a person it seemed in the 1950s impossible to discern what made a Garia a member of society.

EXCHANGING PERSPECTIVES

Seeking the groups by which to specify membership led to much travail. But suppose the problem at which we have arrived were also a fact: suppose Garia conceived the person as a model for relationships. Instead of trying to find the groups of which a person is a member, one would then consider what modeling of relationships the person him- or herself contains. And if Garia society were modeled in the encompassing unity of the singular human being, a person would in this sense not be a part of anything else. A multitude of persons would simply magnify the image of one.

As it turned out, Lawrence placed little weight on jural relations and social cohesion. Instead he emphasized Garia pragmatism and self-interest: 'statements about moral obligation . . . are no more than shorthand terms for considerations of interdependence or mutual self-interest and social survival' (1969: 29). Social conformity, he alarmingly stated, is mere by-product. A relationship valued for the practical and material advantage it confers appears subject to that person's efforts, so that even where expectation is greatest, as among close kin, any sense of indebtedness must be created. Consequently, moral obligation is limited to the circle of effective social ties. Agents thereby play an interpretive role (1984: 195) – it is they who ensure that people 'think on' them.

Lawrence's analysis of pragmatism in the conduct of relations implies no reduction to individualism. On the contrary, relations appear as significant extensions of a person's motivations: others exist in being thought upon (1984: 131 ff). 'Self-regulation' thus indicates the modulation or measuring of relationships by the measure of oneself (1969: 26). Lawrence observed that it operates within the security circle, and thus tautologously with those with whom enduring and effective ties can be demonstrated. Iteanu (1990) offers a similar observation for Orokaiva. People make relationships specific to themselves. External relations are centred on persons as at once subjects and objects of the multiple configuration of their acts, inclinations, and judgements.[5]

In Western terms it would seem a paradox that relationships are not mapped as external connections among a plurality of individuals. Instead, the singularity of the Garia person is conceptualized as a (dividual) figure that encompasses plurality. If in the Garia view there are no relationships that are not submitted to the person's definition of them, then what the person contains is an apprehension of those relations that he or she activates without. If they pre-exist, it is as internal differences within his or her composite body. This, I believe, is also an image of the 'group'. Garia conceptualizations suggest that whatever sociality constitutes the person also constitutes the manner in which relations compose the stock or bush god territories. They are all homologous (Mosko 1985) persons ('beings' [de Coppet 1985]). In this sense, what makes up the part also makes up the whole. As a result, a collectivity such as a cognatic stock is neither an aggregate nor sociality of a different order and can appear equally as one person or as many persons. In the manner, then, in which Garia persons are conceptualized as managing their relations with others, they are the equivalent of all the relationships focused on them.

So what do we do with the recurrent internal division of persons into male and female elements? In their figure of the kindred, focused on a living sibling set with its constellation of maternal and paternal kin, or the bush god territory, focused on an ancestral sibling set with access divided between male- and female-born, Garia conceptualize a composite, androgynous person. I wish to suggest that what distinguishes Garia formulations from the familiar groupings of the so-called lineal systems of their neighbours lies in a temporal modality. What is at issue is the divisive figuring of gender to create a future image of unity.

The point at which persons appear as a composite of male and female elements and the point at which a single gender is definitive are also temporal moments in the reproduction of relations that take a mode imagined across all of Melanesia.[6] Unity emerges once a dual gender identity has been discarded in favour of a single one. The process entails an oscillation between the person conceived as androgynous and the person conceived as single-sex – as groups from elsewhere in Papua New Guinea conceptually shed members of one sex (in marriage) in order to reconceive themselves as one 'person' composed of members of the other. Single-sex persons are presented through the bodies of men or of women or through the mobile female or male items of wealth that pass between them. The decomposition of the composite person thereby reveals the relations, at once internal and external, of which he or she is composed.

Such a Melanesian person – androgynous or single-sex – is not some kind of corporation sole, and the singular person is not conceptualized as a group with relations extrinsic to it. The matrilineal Trobrianders, whom Fortes so eloquently claimed for descent-group theory, present a case in point.

Throughout their lifetimes, Trobrianders activate relationships in a mode that makes the form that every living person takes a composite of maternal and paternal kin. The person can be conceptualized as a vessel, like a canoe containing matrikin, adorned on the outside by its relations with others and especially relations through men. Indeed, the entire kula exchange system is a kind of adornment to matrilineality. At death, the person is divided, and, as Annette Weiner (1976, 1979, 1983) has shown, the descent group achieves unitary form as a collection of ancestral spirits waiting to be reborn. This is a moment at which it appears as a single-sex entity – as it also appears in the images of land or of blood that contain the living body. When it takes after the living person, however, the descent group appears in the form of its numerous extensions and relations to others: land attracts sons to stay, and the foetus is nourished by the father.

Whether external or internal, relations are intrinsic not extrinsic to the living person (Wagner 1991). One might say that relations are what animates the person – vividly imagined in the Trobriand

canoe that speeds across the water because of its masculine attributes towards partners created through paternal and affinal ties. If
relationships give a person life, then at death what is extinguished
are the relationships embodied by the deceased. Indeed, a significant effect of Massim mortuary ceremonies is to strip the deceased
of social ties: the enduring entity is depersonalized. Relationships
created during the lifetime are thus refashioned, for the living can
no longer embody them. In some cases (e.g., Battaglia 1990, Mosko
1989), it is as though people had to recompose the world as it was
before the person existed. But it can only be recomposed in other
persons. The cognatic entity built up during a lifetime is partitioned
at death.

The neighbouring Molima of Fergusson Island (Chowning 1989)
also separate paternal and maternal kin after death. Like the Garia,
the Molima kinship system would have to be called cognatic. Yet
the relative lack of differentiation among consanguines holds only
during an individual's lifetime. At death, the body of kin dissolves
into those whose ties to the deceased are through women and
those whose ties are through men.[7] The kin of the deceased divide
themselves into mourners and workers, each category becoming
conceptually single-sex (as children of a brother, children of a
sister). Yet such a division is a general not a special state of
affairs in Melanesia. It is not that cognatic systems are aberrant[8]
but that everywhere in this part of the world the composite person
is a cognatic system, to be undone or otherwise depluralized,
transformed into a unitary entity at particular moments in time.
It is simply that Molima do not realize their anticipations of this
moment until they assemble to do mortuary service.

In short, what anthropologists have classified as differing principles of Melanesian social organization can also be understood as
an effect of modalities in temporal as well as spatial sequencing.
The mode of dissolution is various, but the 'social organization',
the person, is similarly construed everywhere. To apprehend this,
we need to apprehend the nature of Melanesians' 'perspectivism'.
They live in a world in which perspectives take a particular form,
namely, that of analogies. The result is that perspectives can be
exchanged for one another.

During a lifetime, a singular person exists as an integral part of
relations, if we wish to figure it that way, but only in the sense that
the part is made from the same material as the whole. Relations
also appear as an integral part of persons – the Garia security circle

being managed by people's dispositions, the Trobriand descent group with its outward extensions towards others. What makes the person, then, is no different from what makes up these relations.

Nonetheless, relations appear at different times and in different locations. This is where perspective becomes important. A male member of a matrilineage is both like and unlike a female member, a collectivity of men giving birth to an initiate is both like and unlike a solitary woman in labour, the yams that swell the belly of the Trobriand brother's garden are both like and unlike the yams with which a father feeds his children. There is constant diversification of the forms in which persons and relations appear. Indeed, one may turn into another: my sister is your wife. These are switches of perspective between the positions that persons occupy: donor becomes recipient, daughter's paternal substance becomes mother's maternal substance. A temporal perspective is evident, for instance, in the patrilineal clan groups of the Papua New Guinea Highlands. The groups exist in anticipation of action, the spatial reminders of clan unity – men's house, territorial boundary – expectant of the moment when it will act as one. As one body, one gender, the clan in turn will act to dispose or rearrange the focus of others in relation to it. A clan is thus a transformation of other relations in a specific spacetime (Munn 1986). The 'cognatic' or androgynous person becomes depluralized, decomposed, in the creation of the 'unilinear' single-sex person. Heterogeneous internal relations are thus everted and appear to the agentive clan(sman) as the network of external affines and consanguines it can focus on itself.

In these cases, an oscillation of temporal perspective (before/after) may be imagined as a substitution of external for internal form or of the gender of persons. In the case of gender, a double perspectival move is possible between male and female and between same-sex and cross-sex relations. Yet if these are perspectives they have interesting properties. Instead of providing the bases from which to conceive radically different worlds of knowledge, Melanesian forms allow perspectives to exist at once as analogues and as (potential) transformations of one another, for they contain the possibility that persons can exchange perspectives. My centre is not your centre, but your detached sister/brother (wealth) can be incorporated as the mother/father of my children (my means of reproduction). What is not at issue is that switch of perspective required to perceive an individual as an entity differently constituted from the relationships of which it is part. It is impossible, for instance, to imagine a person cut off from relations and remaining alive (cf. Leenhardt 1979 [1947]). A person is only divested of relations when it no longer embodies them.

In the way that Melanesians present social life to themselves, it would seem that there are no principles of organization that are not also found in the constitution of the person. External relations have the same effect as internal ones. In short, to imagine the person in this manner means that no switch of perspective between person and relations is required in order to 'see' social relations. Exchanging perspectives only differentiates one set of relations from another, as it does one kind of person from another.

COGNATIC KINSHIP?

No more than 'society', however, will this figuring of the person do as a simple cross-cultural category. It is inadequate in turn for grasping the worlds that Euro-Americans imagine for themselves. However, it is an instructive figure with which to conceptualize the difference.

It may seem curious to resurrect British descent-group theory of the midcentury when other – largely continental – formulations of the time were based on the premise that persons have relations integral to them (what else is the specification of the positive marriage rule?), but I do so to remark that at its core was an interesting symbolic device. The nature of the debate that it precipitated over non-unilineal kinship systems reveals in retrospect the character of an indigenous Euro-American kinship system – less in the classification of relations it purported to offer than in the conceptualization of kinship with respect to society. The English are my example, and I take an insider's view.[9]

The matter can be put simply. The English person conceptualized as an individual was in one important sense incomplete (after Carrier n.d.). There always appeared to be 'more than' the person in social life. When the singular person was taken as a unit, relationships involved others as like units. Social life was thus conceptualized as the person's participation in a plurality. As a result, an individual person was only ever a part of some more encompassing aggregate and thereby less than the whole. Where a prototypical Melanesian might have conceptualized the dissolution of the cognatic person as making incomplete an entity already completed by the actions of others, our prototypical English took the person – powerfully symbolized in the child that must be socialized – as requiring completion by society. To focus on the individual person inevitably dissolved this larger category, fragmenting the 'level' at which holism could be seen. Radcliffe-Brown called for the comparison of whole systems because (from the point of view of systems) only systems were whole. The English paradox was that holism was a feature of a part – not the whole – of social life! That is, it was a feature more evident from some (e.g., systemic) perspectives than from others. A particular property of such perspectives was that they appeared either as irreducibly plural or as 'more' or 'less' totalizing or partial.

That the English imagined themselves living between different orders or levels of phenomena, in an incommensurate world of parts and wholes, both created and was itself a precipitate of the manner in which they handled perspective. I have suggested that an example of this way of thinking was evident in the midcentury British debates over cognatic kinship.

Unilineal descent groups were taken as evincing the characteristics of orderly social life. Above all, membership could be demonstrated. Indeed, in their kinship organization, many non-Western peoples seemed to be doing what the anthropologist was also doing in elucidating social structure: classifying according to conventions of social life. The individual person was situated within an order of sociality – descent and succession – whose identity clearly endured beyond the life of any one member. 'Life' as such became an attribute of abstract social systems (Fortes 1958: 1). From the perspective of descent, a group could be conceptualized as a (single) juristic person (Fortes 1969: 304). Yet as we have seen, the same argument assumed that what made individual persons members of a whole group was not what made them whole persons.

Social life was understood as convention. If convention or classification demarcated sociality, then a particular significance seemed to inhere in those parts of the kinship system that regulated the disposition of assets, the loyalty of members, and their own definition as sociocentric entities. Hence the significance of the distinction between 'descent' and 'kinship' and between those (politico-jural) relations that affected group affiliation and those focused on ego as an individual. To the extent that the first set of relations appeared social, the second appeared based on natural connections. The domestic domain was thus seen to deal with reproduction as a biological necessity; there was an internal logic to its own developmental cycle (Mosko 1989), and the network of kin ties focusing on the individual ego appeared a natural ground to other kin conventions. 'Society' and 'nature', we might say, mapped different domains of social relations, the former being more obviously moulded by convention than the latter.[10]

Indeed, consanguineal relations as such indicated a virtual fact of nature, a universalism in human arrangements. There were, it seemed, no societies that, in taking account of parentage, did not take account of the presence of both maternal and paternal kin: 'filiation . . . is universally bilateral' (Fortes 1970 [1953]: 87). Recognition of consanguinity was unremarkable. What varied was the extent to which kin relations were the social basis for group membership. British social anthropology became preoccupied not only with types of descent but with whether peoples had descent groups at all.

It is a pity that the term 'cognatic' should have been so emphatically developed as a complement to the lineal 'agnatic' or 'uterine'.[11] Cognatic ties, wrote Fortes (1970 [1943–4]: 49), are 'ties of actual or assumed physical consanguinity'. For Tallensi, it is in the domestic family that we have

> the sharpest picture of the interaction between cognatic kinship and agnatic ties. We have there the elementary ties of cognatic kinship linking parent to child and sibling to sibling, and we also have the agnatic tie which sets apart the males as the nuclear lineage.
>
> (Fortes 1970 [1943–4]: 50)

Cognatic kinship thus emerged as a kind of ground against which the social relations based on agnation appear. The creation of the latter came to look like the creation of society (out of nature).[12] One may depict it thus: (1) Descent groups exemplified the creation of *social difference* – bounded sociocentric entities cut out of the ramifying networks of individuals. Society was evident in conventional differentiation. (2) The field of cognatic kin thus appeared as a set of consanguines *naturally undifferentiated* – the raw material of kinship. In descent-group systems non-lineal cognates were acknowledged through complementary filiation or the residual claims of subsidiary ties.

The term cognatic was unfortunate if only in that it was in use, and had been for a century (Freeman 1961), for those many other systems in which unilinear descent groups did not exist at all. The prototypes were European as well as English.[13] Without unilinear privilege, each parent was of equal weight and equally differentiated. What became interesting was the effort anthropologists put into redeeming the social significance of kin ties in such societies. The question was how you could both have cognatic systems and have groups. It seemed commonly the case that cognatic kin reckoning coexisted with cutting or bounding classifications that rested on other-than-kinship criteria such as residence (cf. Scheffler 1985). Cognatic systems thus came to have a dual theoretical status, marginalized both in relation to lineal systems and in terms of their own, internal kinship constructs. The latter seemed either thoroughly uninteresting or thoroughly familiar. Interest lay rather in the (non-kinship) conventions by which such systems achieved the kind of closure necessary if they were to be, in the parlance of the time, the building blocks of society.

This focus had been built into kinship studies by the American Morgan. His descriptive systems were a kind of terminological counterpart to cognatic kin reckoning, and ones that purported to describe the world as it was. Such kin terminologies 'correctly' discriminated among given discriminations in the world; in Kuper's (1988: 56) critical comment, they 'mirror[ed] the reality of biological kinship'. After all, terms describing natural differences preserved the uniqueness and particularity of parentage. It was the conventions of other systems that cut the natural facts artificially, classifying relatives in a way that anthropological expertise must then untangle. The 'classificatory' or 'artificial' system certainly did not tell the world as it was. Rather, it 'confound[ed] relationships which, in their nature, are independent and distinct' (Morgan, quoted in Trautmann 1987: 138).

As a result, descriptive systems appeared to display neither artificiality nor convention. If the descriptive system did not need explanation by reference to social convention, its terminologies could be mapped directly onto (natural) relations of consanguinity. To later anthropologists it seemed therefore that one hardly needed social theory to understand it. This was a drastic assumption, for by the mid-twentieth century convention had become the object of study, and the problems for untangling appeared all the other way. Kinship systems that produced groups were no trouble. The trouble with cognatic systems was that tracing cognatic kinship could neither in a strong sense produce groups nor in a weak sense yield a sense of convention or society. Here, in the absence of lineality, was the inverse case: (1) Cognatic kinship reflected *natural difference* in the bilateral reckoning of relations. (2) But the field of cognatic kin was thus *socially undifferentiated* and groups had to be cut out of this field by criteria of a different order.

Society, like the analyses anthropologists produced, was to be made visible in its internal differentiations and categorizations, the social segments it cut from nature. Yet in the cognatic case one saw only the endless recombination of elements devolved from and focusing on individuals. Natural proliferation, ties stretching forever – as Fortes expressed it in his comments on the Garia, there seemed no structure to the mode of kin reckoning itself. Even when kin categories could be identified as focused on sibling pairs or married couples, the result was overlapping and thus incomplete classifications. Conceptualized as a kind of inverse case to lineal holism, the workings of cognatic kinship seemed incapable of yielding a model of a whole.

If 'society' was most visible in groups, it was because they too exemplified classification and convention. Society was held to inhere in the 'level' of organizing principles, not in what was being ordered; levels were literally conceived as of a different order from persons concretely imagined as so many individuals. Hence the central problematic of midcentury anthropology: the relationship between individual and society. Each comprised an irreducible perspective on the other, and the result was pluralism. To think of society rather than to think of the individual was not to exchange perspectives, for there was no reciprocity here. Rather, it was to switch between totalizing worlds. Here each perspective encompassed the other perspective as 'part' of itself.

In this presentation of part-whole relations, the whole was composed of parts, yet the logic of the totality was to be found not in the logic of the individual parts but in organising principles and relations lying beyond them. To perceive life from the perspective of the discrete parts thus yielded a different dimension from the viewpoint gained from the whole. Depending on what was taken as a whole and what was taken as a part, one could always generate (whole) new perspectives and new sets of elements or components. Each part was potentially a whole, but only from other perspectives. Thus an individual person was a potentially holistic entity – but for anthropologists only from the perspective of another discipline such as psychology. From anthropology's own disciplinary perspective, the concept of society stimulated the 'more' holistic vision.

THE VANISHING OF ENGLISH KINSHIP

To argue that the symbolic strategy at the heart of this kinship theorizing was based on the idea that parts cannot be defined by what defines wholes recalls Schneider's (1968) formulation of American kinship. What makes a person a relative, he stated, is not what makes a relative a person. It is to such a switch of perspectives that the kinship constructs of the mid-twentieth century gave facticity and certainty. What was embedded in anthropological kinship thinking was, I suspect, reflected back by the folk models of the 'wider society' of which it was a part.

Now, while I take 'English' as my exemplar of a folk model and thus illustrative of Euro-American kinship thinking, there is also good reason to suppose that the trivialization of kinship in social life is a characteristic that may well distinguish it from some continental or southern European models (though may give it an affinity to aspects of 'American' kinship). It is of interest insofar as it has helped shape British anthropological theorizing on kinship. Both belong to a cultural era I have called modernist or pluralist.

The short question is why a Western kinship system of the English kind has been so hard to conceptualize theoretically. Part of the answer must lie in conceptualizing it as cognatic, for that meant it became profoundly uninteresting. Either its mode of kinship reckoning is entirely unproblematic because it self-evidently follows natural distinctions or it is entirely problematic because it solves so few of the other questions we would ask about social life. It disappears in studies of local communities or class or visiting patterns. We have a feeling that kinship in English society ought to have a significant social dimension, despite the fact that all we can see is the number of times daughters visit their mothers or who gets what at Christmas. But what we then 'see' is the incompleteness of kinship as an explanatory device. We have to reintroduce dimensions of class and income and neighbourhood, and our grasp of what might be distinctive about kinship has again vanished.

That the English cannot pin down a sense of society when they reflect on their own kinship system is an artefact of the system itself, and that is because of the way it makes kinship vanish. Collaterals do not, of course, go on forever; they fade out rather quickly (Firth, Hubert, and Forge 1969: 170–1), but not for reasons to do with the nature of the kin connection. Other factors intervene, and this is the point. Kinship seems less than a complete system. 'Kinship and marriage', Fox (1967: 27) writes, 'are about the basic facts of life. They are about "birth, and copulation, and death"'. But birth and copulation and death are not about society. Rather, they chart the individual person's movement 'through' it. Fox expresses this commonsense disjunction in an unremarked shift of phrase: 'Birth produces children. . . . death produces a gap in the social group'.

From a British view, then, despite our best efforts as anthropologists to see our own conventions, we somehow take the manner in which the English trace kin along lines of consanguinity as socially trivial. Society lies 'beyond' kinship, impinging as a different order of phenomena. But suppose that this problem were also fact: suppose that this incompleteness were part of English kinship thinking. Instead of trying to specify what the social significance of kinship might be, we would consider what modeling of plurality kinship formulations themselves contain. Let me rephrase the modeling at issue and reinstate the tense that indicates the temporal perspective from which I write.

What I have called modernist or pluralist in this kinship thinking produced the figure of the person as an individual, made up of the physical materials that made up other individuals but recombining them in a unique way. In this sense, the person was a whole individual. But what made the person a whole individual was not what made him or her a part of any wider identity. In relation to society, the individual was incomplete – to be completed *by* socialization, relationships and convention. The problematic at the heart of midcentury British anthropology was also a proposition at the heart of twentieth-century English kinship.

The proposition neatly encapsulated the manner in which anthropologists produced plural and fragmented worlds for themselves as much as it did the manner in which they produced totalizing and holistic ones. The moment one switched from looking at a person as a unique individual to his or her relations with others, one added a dimension of another order. Each perspective might be used to totalizing effect, yet each totalizing perspective was vulnerable to other perspectives that made its own purchase on reality incomplete. The individual person was both a part of society and a part of nature. Society both was cut out of nature and encapsulated nature within itself. To switch from one perspective to another was to switch whole domains of explanation. The parts were not equal, since perspectives could not matched. They overlapped; one whole was only a part of another. Thus social convention could be conceptualized as modifying and encompassing natural givens; and what made up the elements of a narrative was not conceptualized as the narrative itself.

This was evinced in the biology of procreation and death. A child was endowed with material from both parents, literally formed from parts of them. Yet it was regarded as equivalent to neither mother nor father nor to the relation between them: rather, it was a hybrid product in another sense, a genetically unique individual with a life of its own. It was only a part of their life, despite the fact that its genetic material was formed wholly from theirs. On the other hand, at death, what gave the individual uniqueness was left as the acts and relations exercised during the lifetime – the individual person only borrowed a part of life itself. Like society, life would carry on. So now life was part of the individual person, now the individual was a part of life: life and person overlapped but did not match. Built into this conceptualization was a generative incompleteness. If genetic endowment must be complemented by environment and nurture, there was no sense in which a kinperson could stand for a social totality.

A consequence of such thinking was that once a foetus was created through the recombination of genetic elements, that conception could not be undone. Similarly, a person always retained social identity, as an individual with a life history, and this remained true after death. Death did not take away the individuality of the person. What it did, though, was take away life.

Life was regarded, then, as larger than the person who embodied it. The deceased was colloquially 'cut off' from a stream of existence that was more than him or her, as he or she was cut off from an active part in social relationships. Death terminated the enjoyment of relations such as marriage that remained thereafter frozen in the record (cf. Wolfram 1987: 213). People also spoke of persons in their lifetime 'cut off' from society, or even 'cut off' from their kin – by which they meant not the undoing of genetic inheritance but separation from a domain of sociability. Indeed, 'rootlessness' applied to persons signified less a change in the nature of physical attachment to others than the state of being cut off from a community of persons, typically from home. Kin could thus be seen as a kind of community, a background from which the striving individual might seek to depart.

The kinperson, in this midcentury view, recombined genetic material in irreversible sequence. But when he or she was thought of as cut out of something, that something appeared as a metaphysical entity of a different order of reality from the person: society, home, even life itself. In fact, death most concretely indicated that whatever it was that the individual person belonged to in his or her lifetime, it was only the individual deceased who ceased to be part of it; that other something continued.

Such modernist perspectives had their own pluralizing effect. When perspectives cannot be exchanged, one perspective can only capture the essence of another by encapsulating it as a part of itself. Parts in turn thus always appear to be cut from other, larger wholes. But if perspectives cannot be imagined at all, what then?

POST-PLURAL VISIONS

Some people in the West think they now live in a world that has lost the unifying perspective of modernism. This leaves the problem of what to do with parts and wholes. I offer an American example.

I have been struck by the organizing images of Clifford's *The Predicament of Culture* (1988) – his concern with the rootlessness that offcentres persons and scatters traditions. This mood of lost authenticity – the idea that the world is full of changed, part-cultures – is not new. What is new (he says) is the setting that the late twentieth century provides: 'a truly global space of cultural connections and dissolutions has become imaginable: local authenticities meet and merge in transient . . . settings' (1988: 4). The problem is how to respond to an unprecedented overlay of traditions. Ethnography must be an ethnography of conjunctures, moving between cultures, a cosmopolitan practice which participates in the hybridization he sees everywhere. Yet (he argues) ethnographies have always been composed of cut-outs, bits extracted from context, brought together in analysis and narrative. What is also new is the way we think about the hybridization. Texts that once celebrated the integration of cultural artefacts have been displaced by deliberate attention to the uniqueness of fragments. Creativity can only lie in their recombination. Clifford sees this as a salvation not just for texts but for the concept of culture itself, for cultures have always been hybrids, 'the roots of tradition [forever] cut and retied' (1988: 15). Tradition?

The therapeutic hope of his own efforts is for the 'reinvention of difference' (1988: 15). Elements cut from diverse times and places can be recombined, though they cannot fit together as a whole. He back-projects the supposition that they never did, so he is left with another problem, which is what on earth they have been cut *from*. Distinctive ways of being still exist despite their hybrid manifestations, and he evokes the shadowy presence of some other dimension, rather like a lost perspective. Now, Clifford is coy about characterizing this dimension – this realm of an order different from the individual fragments yet from which the fragments have come. No doubt he is coy for the reason that his predecessors have been certain, for he does not want to reconceptualize a totalizing whole.

Clifford's problem, then, is not that of simple multiplicity or of the multiculturalism of contact. Rather, it is post-plural vision of a composite world forever the result of borrowings and interchanges. In his view, such a habitation significantly resists the global vision of (say) Lévi-Strauss's *Tristes tropiques* (1955), with its 1950s nostalgia for authentic human differences disappearing in an expansive commodity culture. Rather than being placed at the end of the world's many histories, the European narrative of a progressive monoculture is to be set beside the creolization of culture itself. He evokes the Caribbean: a history of degradation, mimicry, violence but one that is also rebellious, syncretic, and creative. Without wholes, the only thing to do is recombine the parts.

Listen, then, to how the images of recombination and cutting work. Listen to what happens when one imagines Clifford's vision of the post-modern world as though he were thinking kinship of the English kind.

Clifford's criticism is of those who mistook people's collections for the representation of a collective life: there never were any authentic indigenous master narratives for which the anthropologist's master narrative was an appropriate genre. The classifier of ethnographic collections 'invents' a relationship between artefact and culture. Cut out of their (living) contexts, artefacts are made to stand for abstract wholes, a Bambara mask for Bambara culture. Creolization, by contrast, makes incongruity evident, as in ethnographies which leave 'the cuts and sutures of the research process' visible (1988: 146). Ethnography as collage 'would be an assemblage containing voices other than the ethnographer's, as well as examples of "found" evidence, data not fully integrated within the work's governing interpretation' (1988: 147). Here is the potential creativity of ethnography. Rather than the creativity of convention, of human kinship 'reduced to discrete differential systems' (1988: 241), ethnography must remain open to registering the original act of combination – the procreation of a hybrid.

Clifford's presentation of cultures as bits and pieces cut up and recombined contains borrowings of its own. On the one hand, like rootless persons cultures are always in fragments; on the other hand, in their collecting it is past anthropologists who have cut up cultures into the bits reassembled in their narratives. Cultures are always hybrids, yet cultural future lies in further creative recombining, including the recombinations of the ethnographic enterprise. As Clifford depicts the late-twentieth-century ethnography, its skilled differentiations will apply to differences already there. He quotes Said: 'A part of something is for the foreseeable future going to be better than all of it. Fragments over wholes. . . . To tell your story in pieces, *as it is*' (1988: 11).

This is the old reproductive idiom of biological kinship. Clifford does not, of course, talk kinship. Yet transmuted into his language of ethnographic creativity are, I suggest, ideas equally applicable to midcentury notions of procreation. Persons are natural hybrids: the creative recombination of already differentiated genetic material makes everyone a new entity. The past might have been collected into ancestral traditions, but the future lies in perpetual hybridization.

That genetic analogy was not available to Morgan, but the manner in which Morgan's descriptive systems distinguish own parents from collateral relatives emphasizes the particulate state of each individual. The particularity of parentage is the guarantee (cf. Schneider 1984). Thus genealogical trees appropriately focus on ego, the individual repository of inheritances recombined from other persons, each in turn unique. It was this particularism that classificatory terminological systems with their artificial conventions failed to describe. If there was a sense in which descriptive terminologies seemed self-evident to Morgan, I see a devolved parallel with Clifford's late-twentieth-century vision. Clifford finds it unproblematic to convey the hybridization of a hybrid world, with its particulate nature and unique moments. Yet hybrids are not to be stabilized as wholes. For him, all the 'problems' lie in those master narratives which purported to reveal holistic societies – in which case the real problem lies in being heir to them and thus to its supposition that parts are always cut from something else: how to conceptualize a part that is not a part of a whole?

From Morgan to Clifford might seem a bizarre genealogy, but these figures are useful bookends. Morgan belonged to an era that had just finished debating whether humankind had one or many origins; Clifford speaks for a world that has ceased to see either unity or plurality in an unambiguous way. What lies between are years of modernist scholarship with its vision of a plurality of cultures and societies whose comparison rested on the unifying effect of this or that governing perspective. Each perspective simultaneously pluralized the subject matter of anthropological study and held out the promise of a holistic understanding that would show elements fitted together and parts completed.

At least for British anthropology, I suspect it was a similar intimacy between anthropological and folk models that in fact made the indigenous system impossible to analyse; it either appeared as a negative version of other kinship systems or was universalized as displaying the facts that others tried to conventionalize. Such conventions were found in societies where kinship seemed central to the manner in which society itself was represented. 'Kinship' was, of course, already conceptualized as a 'system', and systems were seen to be wholes made up of (interdependent) parts. But to give 'parts' their distinct identity would draw one into other perspectives, other totalizing systems of relations. In Western society one could take the perspective of kinship, but this could not also be the perspective of society.

In anthropological discourse, systems, like conventions or like societies and cultures, were frequently personified as agents with interests of their own – an image laminated in the depiction of corporate groups as juristic persons. But perhaps Clifford does more than reconceptualize an old procreative model. His post-plural vision repersonifies relationships as a living hybrid of forms, so that all that is visible is culture itself – the grafting process of cultivating new growth from previous material. Perhaps his vocabulary also looks forward to a new kinship that will have to deal with transgenic life forms and the mapping of the human genome in the interest of therapy. If so, it is a vocabulary suffused with nostalgia for an unproblematic holism.

Think again of the Garia person. It was a fancy, of course, ever to have supposed that this Melanesian figure contains an image of 'society', for the very idea of society in Western thinking entailed an encompassment of perspectives. Society did not in Garia modeling provide a perspective on the singular person any more than the singular person provided a perspective on society. There was in that sense no perspective, or, rather, only the one perspective, from the centre, of which others were always analogies or transformations. Thus to imagine another person was to exchange perspectives: one person's periphery appeared as another person's centre (Werbner n.d.). But is one perspective not also a loss of perspectives? Whatever insight a post-plural vision might yield here, Garia nostalgia is unlikely to be of the English or American kind.

New dismantling idioms might give anthropologists a vocabulary with which to apprehend other people's dismantling projects, but 'our' project should not be mistaken for 'theirs'. We are not devolved from and do not reproduce the same worlds.

Parallels between 'Melanesian' and 'Western' or Euro-American conceptualizations always were elusive. The Garia security circle looked at first blush like the ramifying kin network of consanguines with which many Europeans were familiar. Yet the figure of the Garia person was never a genetic hybrid, complete by inheritance and endowment but incomplete when thought of as a part of a wider society. Rather, socially complete, it was made incomplete in its engagement and exchange with others. Nor did the holism of Melanesian imagery mean that Melanesians did not envision cutting. On the contrary, images of partition, extraction, severance were commonplace. Differentiation was a principal preoccupation (see, e.g., James Weiner 1988): male from female, donor from recipient, the protocols were endless. But what was 'cut' were persons and relations themselves: person from person, relation from relation, not persons cut off from relations. Far from being fixed in time at the moment of birth, relations were the active life on which the person was forever working.

What differentiated relations in Melanesia was the exchange of people's perspectives on one another: the transfer of valuables that guaranteed that a woman would bear her husband's child and not her father's or the work of spouses in procreation that must be repeated before birth and supplemented by nurture afterwards. A person was created, so to speak, out of the same materials by which it created its own life: composite but not unique, 'cut' and partitioned but not from a sphere external to it. The Highlands woman being prepared for marriage might be both severed from her clan and internally divided – detached from and made to void paternal substance. Everything was partible.[13] But this partitioning did not create different orders of being out of parts and wholes.

The modernist imagery of parts and wholes worked to different effect, and it is to this that we are heir. It made us see persons as parts cut from a whole imagined as relations, life, and, for the anthopologist, society. Conversely, in the discourse of systems and structures it was relations, life, society that creatively recombined the fragments and parts. The 'cognatic kinship' of Western society reproduced unique individuals whose procreation was perpetually modified by an overlay of other principles of social life. Take the individual away and, English would say, society will still endure. But a Melanesian death required the active severance of persons and relations – living persons rearranging their relationships among themselves when the deceased could no longer embody them. This included 'undoing' the cognatic ties which constituted life.

What was creative about the recombinations that Melanesians enacted – the wealth and children they made – was that they antici- pated and were made of acts similar to those which subsequently partitioned them. Parts were never dislocated in this sense, left on the cutting-room floor, so to speak, to be recombined by someone else. Contrary to understood wisdom, Melanesians have never needed salvage ethnography. Their vision of the world had no problem with how parts fit together. There were no bits and pieces that had to be put back again, for the sake of a culture to restore, a society to conceptualize. Saved Clifford's predicament, I doubt that nostalgia for either culture or society figures in their present cosmopolitanism.

NOTES

1 For instance, Thornton argues that much of the significance of 'society' lay in its power as a rhetorical trope for the organization of anthropological data. Positing analytical components capable of theoretical integration presumed an entirety to the object of study as a whole made up of parts, so that society emerged as a holistic precipitate of analysis. '[T]he imagination of wholes is a rhetorical

imperative for ethnography since it is this image of wholeness that gives the ethnography a sense of fulfilling "closure" that other genres accomplish by different rhetorical means' (1988: 286). Conversely, 'it may be that it is impossible to conceptualize society, except in terms of holistic images' (p. 298). Analysis in turn became the decomposition of an imagined whole. Outside the Dumontian tradition, much of the convincing character of society as a whole derived from the equally convincing representation of parts ('subsystems') that could be further subdivided into parts.

2 It reworks material that has appeared or will appear elsewhere, in memorial essays for Peter Lawrence (1988b) and Ralph Bulmer (to be edited by A. Pawley, Auckland). I thank Adam Kuper for conceptualizing the whole problem and to Daniel de Coppet for persuading me to take part. An earlier version was given in Manchester, and I am grateful for my colleagues' many comments, as I am to Debbora Battaglia, James Carrier, and Mark Mosko.

3 While Fortes (1970 [1953]: 81) allowed himself to refer to a 'society made up of corporate lineages', it was an image that later he took great pains to undo (e.g., 1969: 287). On the disjunction between Fortes's own rich documentation of the Tallensi case (including their overlapping fields of clanship) and his theoretical axioms, see Kuper (1982: 85), and for a similar point with regard to the relationship of 'descent' and 'group', see Scheffler (1985: 9).

4 I do not make here a distinction offered elsewhere (1988a: chap. 10), between persons as the objects of relations and agents who act in respect of persons/relations.

5 What renders the so-called lineal systems distinct is the way in which relations engaged in the lifetime are regarded as making the complete lineage person 'incomplete' – the person is restored to a final completeness (a state of pre-procreation) at death.

6 On Molima, the mortuary rearrangements of persons are permanent but cannot take place in advance; elsewhere they are anticipated and may even be acted upon in premortuary exchanges finalized at death. In the Papua New Guinea Highlands, birth is the prominent event in relation to which people dispose themselves, entailing the fresh affirmation of relations on a categorical basis, above all the distinction between the child's paternal and maternal kin.

7 'Cognatic systems' crop up all over Melanesia with disconcerting randomness. Molima themselves live in a region dominated by 'matrilineal' descent, and I capitalize on Chowning's consistent scepticism about the utility of correlating types of descent with other features of social organization – most recently expressed in her remark that Massim studies have tended to focus on unilineal groups as though maintaining them were the central concern of their members.

8 I have since read Bouquet's (n.d.) account of English kinship mediated by her teaching of British Social Anthropology in Portugal. The educated, middle-class 'English' taken as my reference point are defended as a category in a longer work of my own (n.d.).

9 Note the construction. A discriminating axis that separates one domain from another reappears as a distinction internal to one or other domain. Fortes does this to Morgan's distinction between *societas* and *civitas*: modes of public life that discriminate whole evolutionary epochs are reconceptualized as spheres or domains of relations within a single society (see the critique in Mosko 1989).

10 Although the concept 'residual' was always used in a strictly relative sense, the impression is that cognatic ties were of secondary significance: however important non-lineal ties were for the individual person, they could not in this view carry sociocentric significance.

11 Fox (1967: 172), in reference to various types of cognatic kindred: 'Obviously the system of cognatic kindreds rings a bell for most readers as it resembles our own kinship system which is, however, unformalized and lacks named kindreds'. Conversely, Fortes (1969: 309, my emphasis): 'I regard it as now established that the elementary components of patrifiliation and matrifiliation, and hence of agnatic, enatic, and cognatic modes of reckoning kinship are, *like genes in the individual organism* invariably present in all familial systems'.

12 Freeman (1961: 200) lists those who, in the 1950s, were developing the term 'kindred' in the sense that European jurists had long used it (to refer to all of an individual's cognates).

13 Where persons are cut from persons (or relations from relations), as we might imagine a female agnate severed from her clan or donor distinguished from recipient, then one position or perspective is substituted for another of comparable order. Thus Molima substitute the division of maternal and paternal kin at death for their combination in the living person. When persons die, they become reconstituted as siblings – their marriages, so to speak, undone and their children deconceived. Now, insofar as one set of relations (siblingship) substitutes for another (conjugality), it is also anticipated, and in that sense 'already there'. How different from the novelty with which English kinship (say) perceives the natural creation of individual persons and the social creation of relations!

REFERENCES

Battaglia, Debbora (1990) *On the Bones of the Serpent: Person, Memory, and Mortality in Sabarl Island Society*, Chicago: University of Chicago Press.

Bloch, Maurice (1986) *From Blessing to Violence: History and Ideology in the Circumcision Ritual of the Merina of Madagascar*, Cambridge: Cambridge University Press.

Bouquet, Mary (n.d.) *Pedigree: Reclaiming English Kinship*, Manchester: Manchester University Press. In press.

Carrier, James (n.d.) 'Cultural content and practical meaning: the construction of symbols in formal American culture', MS.

Chowning, Ann (1989) 'Death and kinship in Molima', in F. Damon and R. Wagner (eds) *Death Rituals and Life in the Societies of the Kula Ring*, De Kalb: Northern Illinois University Press.

Clifford, James (1988) *The Predicament of Culture: Twentieth-Century Ethnography, Literature, and Art*, Cambridge, MA: Harvard University Press.

Coppet, Daniel de (1981) 'The life-giving death', in S. C. Humphreys and H. King (eds) *Mortality and Immortality: The Anthropology and Archaeology of Death*, London: Academic Press.

——(1985) 'Land owns people', in R. H. Barnes, D. de Coppet, and R. J. Parkin (eds) *Contexts and Levels: Anthropological Essays on Hierarchy*, Oxford: JASO.

Damon, Frederick (1989) 'The Muyuw *lo'un* and the end of marriage', in F. Damon and R. Wagner (eds) *Death Rituals and Life in the Societies of the Kula Ring*, De Kalb: Northern Illinois University Press.

Firth, Raymond, Hubert, Jane and Forge, Anthony (1969) *Families and Their Relatives: Kinship in a Middle-Class Sector of London*, London: Routledge and Kegan Paul.

Fortes, Meyer (1958) 'Introduction' in J. Goody (ed.) *The Developmental Cycle in Domestic Groups*, Cambridge: Cambridge University Press.

——(1969) *Kinship and the Social Order*, Chicago: Aldine.

——(1970) *Time and Social Structure, and Other Essays*, London: Athlone Press.

——(1984) 'Foreword', in Peter Lawrence, *The Garia*, Melbourne: Melbourne University Press.

Fox, Robin (1967) *Kinship and Marriage: An Anthropological Perspective*, Harmondsworth: Penguin.

Freeman, Derek (1961) 'On the concept of the kindred', *Journal of Royal Anthropological Institute* 91: 192–220.

Gillison, Gillian (1991) 'The flute myth and the law of equivalence: origins of a principle of exchange', in M. Godelier and M. Strathern (eds) *Big Men and Great Men: Personifications of Power in Melanesia*, Cambridge: Cambridge University Press.

Hannerz, Ulf (1988) 'American culture: creolized, creolizing', in Erik Åsard (ed.) *American Culture: Creolized, Creolizing, and Other Lectures from the NAAS Biennial Conference in Uppsala, May 28–31, 1987*, Uppsala: Swedish Institute for North American Studies.

——(1990) 'Cosmopolitans and locals in world culture', *Theory, Culture, and Society* 7: 211–25.

Iteanu, André (1990) 'The concept of the person and the ritual system: an Orokaiva view', *Man*, n.s., 25: 35–53.

Kuper, Adam (1982) 'Lineage theory: a critical retrospect', *Annual Review of Anthropology* 11: 71–95.

——(1988) *The Invention of Primitive Society: Transformations of an Illusion*, London: Routledge.

Lawrence, Peter (1969) 'The state versus stateless societies in Papua New Guinea', in B. J. Brown (ed.) *Fashion of Law in New Guinea*, Sydney: Butterworths.

——(1971) 'The Garia of the Madang District', in R. M. Berndt and P. Lawrence (eds) *Politics in New Guinea*, Nedlands: University of Western Australia Press.

——(1984) *The Garia: An Ethnography of a Traditional Cosmic System in Papua New Guinea*, Melbourne: Melbourne University Press.

Leenhardt, Maurice (1979 [1947]) *Do Kamo: Person and Myth in the Melanesian World*, trans. B. M. Gulati, Chicago: University of Chicago Press.

Lévi-Strauss, Claude (1955) *Tristes tropiques*, Paris: Plon.

Mosko, Mark (1985) *Quadripartite Structure: Categories, Relations, and Homologies in Bush Mekeo Culture*, Cambridge: Cambridge University Press.

——(1989) 'The developmental cycle among public groups', *Man*, n.s., 24: 470–84.

Munn, Nancy D. (1986) *The Fame of Gawa: A Symbolic Study of Value Transformation in a Massim (Papua New Guinea) Society*, Cambridge: Cambridge University Press.

Radcliffe-Brown, A. R. (1950) 'Introduction', in A. R. Radcliffe-Brown and D. Forde (eds) *African Systems of Kinship and Marriage*, London: Oxford University Press.

——(1952) *Structure and Function in Primitive Society*, London: Cohen and West.

Radcliffe-Brown, A. R. and Forde, D. (eds) (1950) *African Systems of Kinship and Marriage*, London: Oxford University Press.

Scheffler, Harold W. (1985) 'Filiation and affiliation', *Man*, n.s., 20: 1–21.

Schneider, David M. (1968) *American Kinship: A Cultural Account*, Englewood Cliffs: Prentice-Hall.

——(1984) *A Critique of the Study of Kinship*, Ann Arbor: University of Michigan Press.

Strathern, Marilyn (1988a) *The Gender of the Gift: Problems with Women and Problems with Society in Melanesia*, Berkeley and Los Angeles: University of California Press.

——(1988b) 'Self-regulation: an interpretation of Peter Lawrence's writing on social control', *Oceania* 59: 3–6.

——(n.d.) *After Nature*, Cambridge: Cambridge University Press. In press.

Thornton, Robert (1988) 'The rhetoric of ethnographic holism', *Cultural Anthropology* 3: 285–303.

Trautmann, Thomas R. (1987) *Lewis Henry Morgan and the Invention of Kinship*, Berkeley and Los Angeles: University of California Press.

Wagner, Roy (1986) *Asiwinarong: Ethos, Image, and Social Power among the Usen Barok of New Ireland*, Princeton: Princeton University Press.

——(1991) 'The fractal person', in M. Godelier and M. Strathern (eds) *Big Men and Great Men: Personifications of Power in Melanesia*, Cambridge: Cambridge University Press.

Weiner, Annette B. (1976) *Women of Value, Men of Renown: New Perspectives in Trobriand Exchange*, Austin: University of Texas Press.

——(1979) 'Trobriand kinship from another view: the reproductive power of women and men', *Man*, n.s., 14: 328–48.

——(1983) '"A world of made is not a world of born": Doing kula in Kiriwina', in J. W. Leach and E. R. Leach (eds) *The Kula: New Perspectives on Massim Exchange*, Cambridge: Cambridge University Press.

Weiner, James F. (1988) *The Heart of the Pearlshell: The Mythological Dimension of Foi Sociality*, Berkeley and Los Angeles: University of California Press.

Werbner, Richard P. (n.d.) 'Trickster and the eternal return: self-reference in West Sepik world renewal', in B. Juillerat (ed.) *The Mother's Brother is the Breast: Ritual and Meaning in the West Sepik*, Washington, D. C.: Smithsonian Institution. In press.

Wolfram, Sybil (1987) *In-laws and Outlaws: Kinship and Marriage in England*, London: Croom Helm.

Part III

Models of society, the individual, and nature

Chapter 5

Societies of nature and the nature of society

Philippe Descola

Conceptualizing society, the anthropologist confronts a paradoxical problem. Ever since Malinowski, a strong tradition, embodied in influential monographs, has encouraged ethnographers to describe small-scale and territorially circumscribed pre-literate groups as if they were perfectly coherent totalities, each endowed with a particular cultural logic which, properly decoded, offers a key for interpreting the observations recorded day after day. Yet many ethnographers would admit that the members of the societies they study do not spontaneously picture their cultures as systematic wholes. Rather, they haphazardly combine partial points of view and elicited intuitions, scraps of knowledge and appeals to tradition, to produce – unknowingly and collectively – something approximating to the global image mirrored by the monograph. True, some native exegetes have been known to produce systematic syntheses, but they are so few that most anthropology students know their names. Furthermore, the knowledge imparted by these exceptional informants often stems from a very personal vision of the world or from highly esoteric teachings which are by no means generally known or appreciated.

This obvious and often underscored mismatch of perspectives between observer and observed and even between differently situated informants raises two questions, distinct methodologically but epistemologically closely linked. The first concerns the status of ethnography: Can the synthetic totality constructed by an ethnographer as a result of fieldwork be anything other than an *ad hoc* interpretive model of the society studied? Can it do more than simply communicate one person's patiently acquired experience of a single culture, more or less felicitously depending on the literary skills of the ethnographer and the quality of his observations? As for the anthropological problem, it logically follows from the preceding question: Can anthropology, as a science of the variability of cultures, depend upon such heterogeneous interpretive models to achieve its programme?

To state the problem in such terms is to invite a negative answer. It is implausible that an explanatory theory of cultural differences could be rigorously inferred from a comparison of interpretive constructs which have nothing in common beyond an approximate conformity to the narrative conventions of ethnographic monographs. The incoherences and failures of an inductive approach which would found anthropological reasoning upon a collation of ethnographic points of view have led some anthropologists to confess their impotence, which the more philosophically minded among them may prefer to call relativism. The process is familiar: rather than question the legitimacy of a type of knowledge or a mode of conceptualization of knowable objects, the relativist prefers to argue that the means and meanings of knowledge itself are culturally heterogeneous. The relativist is condemned to oscillate between the impasses of radical solipsism and the contradictions of an eclectic psychology. Dan Sperber has accurately pinpointed the aporias and metaphysical presuppositions inherent in the kind of 'cognitive apartheid' advocated by relativism (1982: 179). I need not therefore expand on a critical analysis to which I fully subscribe, and which has its source in a rationalist tradition shared by most French anthropologists.

But if anthropologists reject the relativist point of view, the problem it was intended to deny must be confronted. How, then, are we to conceptualize society? Certainly not by pursuing an inductive comparison of empirical objects, each given an artificial unity by the holistic interpretation of its ethnographer, or by dissolving society into a mere aggregate, the cumulative product of individual transactions and conflicting interests. If anthropology is to have a future outside of *belles-lettres*, it must deal with the principles of the construction of reality. Somehow the totality produced by an ethnographer must be made credible and the behaviour described by another rendered comprehensible.

I will start with the hypothesis that such principles of order are rooted in overarching schemes through which each culture organizes its practices in an immediately distinctive pattern. Schemes of praxis are not intuitively given: as Claude Lévi-Strauss has suggested, they can only be deduced from the results of their operation. These products are not themselves institutions, sets of values, cosmologies, or even systems of social relations: they are realized as structures, 'at once empirical and intelligible beings', which defy direct observation and must be reconstructed by an analytical effort (Lévi-Strauss 1962a: 173). By taking on the task of isolating schemes of praxis and elaborating a theory of their differential effects, anthropology may hope to escape its present subjection to ethnography and to confer scientific legitimacy on this essentially intuitive mode of interpreting otherness. The existence of such structures may also help to explain the correspondence – which is usually presupposed – between the image of coherence perceived and built up by the observer and the relative consistency that can be discerned in acts and statements even though the actors themselves are generally unable, except by way of fragmentary allusions, to relate them to an explicit model of the society and the world. Anthropological theory, and therefore comparison, would then deal not with interpretive totalities or individual strategies but with the principles which order them.[1]

THE OBJECTIFICATION OF NATURE AND OF OTHERNESS

Though it may appear unduly ambitious, this conception of anthropology has respectable antecedents, and its potential has been made apparent by such scholars as Claude Lévi-Strauss, Gregory Bateson, Georges Dumézil, and Louis Dumont. Each has contributed in his own sphere and with his own characteristic methods to the project of an explanatory theory of the variability of cultural phenomena, the goal being the elucidation of the deep structures that regulate ideologies and behaviours.

Certain domains of social practice are better suited to this task than others. One such concerns the objectification of nature. The basic importance of this field has long been recognized by several otherwise largely conflicting tendencies in contemporary anthropology. The sustained concern with the modes of use and representation of the natural environment which has united structuralists, Marxists, ethnoscientists, and cultural ecologists is obviously not reducible to a mere fashion, and although it has generated countless misunderstandings this unplanned convergence of interest reveals a common, albeit rarely explicit, assumption: the principles of the construction of social reality are primarily to be sought in the relations between human beings and their natural environment.

There are good grounds for supposing that the social objectification of nature is implemented through a limited number of
operative schemes. The first derives from comparative studies of
native systems of classification of fauna and flora. If, as appears
more and more probable, all folk taxonomies of natural objects
are governed by identical mental procedures, it is not unreasonable
to suppose that the modes of representation of the interactions
between human beings and nature are themselves supported by a
few cognitive universals, particularly those that order the semantics
of 'life-forms' (Berlin, Breedlove, and Raven 1973). Admittedly,
there is a huge gap between the probable universality of the
principles which underlie these folk taxonomies and the empirical
diversity of symbolic organizations of the world. However, without
taking sides in the nature/nurture controversy, an epistemologically
coherent anthropology might appeal to the existence of cognitive
devices which are shared by all in support of an attempt to
elaborate a grammar of the variety of ways in which nature is
socialized.

It would, however be dangerous to assume that the schemes
which regulate relations between human beings and their environment must spring from a limited (and largely unexplored) set
of mental constraints. This might even suggest a reversion to the
speculations of an obsolete idealism. These relations obviously
change as technical systems and forms of production evolve – a
cumulative process which constantly reveals new uses and new
properties of a nature more and more transformed by social
practice. The taxonomic hierarchies of natural objects remain
constant, but the representations of the *relations* of people to these
objects undergo periodic reorganization, generally imperceptible
to those who experience them but sufficiently significant in the
long run to impose a kind of rhythm on the course of human
history.[2]

It is therefore not enough to recognize that ideas about the
interaction between a community and its environment probably
derive ultimately from notions which are rooted in human cognitive processes. Each specific form of cultural conceptualization
also introduces sets of rules governing the use and appropriation
of nature, evaluations of technical systems, and beliefs about
the structure of the cosmos, the hierarchy of beings, and the
very principles by which living things function. The logic which
informs these configurations is dictated both by the characteristics

of the ecosystems to which each culture must adapt itself and by the types of practice through which these ecosystems are socialized. Nevertheless, the variety of such systems is not infinite. The environment of each human group is in principle different from that of all others, so it is virtually impossible to compile a comprehensive diachronic inventory of human ecosystems; but the schemes that organize the socialization of these ecosystems are undoubtedly far less diversified than the objects to which they apply. They may also differ widely between societies in similar types of physical environment. In other words, there is no predictable correspondence between specific ecosystems and specific schemes of praxis. As 'nature' is always constructed by reference to the human domain, these schemes are ultimately informed by ideas and practices concerning 'self' and 'otherness'. There is a homology between the way in which we address 'nature' and the way in which we address 'others'.

This idea is not entirely new, and it may be discerned in the technical determinism to which Marx occasionally yields[3] and which some of his followers have incautiously fostered. The guiding notion here is that the social relations characteristic of an economic period are ultimately determined by the modes of exploitation of nature – nature being treated as the passive material upon which human creativity goes to work. This is a perspective which clashes with Marx's classical doctrine – that the differentiation of modes of production is determined by the social relations of production and not by the productive forces. Empirically, moreover, new social forms are not necessarily or simply triggered by technical changes. There are many instances in which techniques of production were known and even in use in a marginal way but could not fully be put to work without a prior reorganization of social relations.

A more fruitful hypothesis was suggested some years ago by Haudricourt (1962). The Neolithic Revolution, he argued, brought about a radical transformation in the relations between humans and nature. Human beings were led to establish bonds of affective coexistence with the species that they had domesticated, bonds of the same order as those prevailing within the social sphere. Haudricourt instanced the contrast between what he called indirect negative action and direct positive action, modes of social action operating both within society and with respect to nature. Indirect negative action can be illustrated by the technique of yam cultivation as it is practised in New Caledonia: brutal treatment of the plants is excluded in favour of minute preparation of the ground where each plant is to grow. Whereas Western cereals are collectively submitted to violent operations, tropical roots and tubers elicit an individualized and 'respectful friendship' which finds its parallel in Melanesian political conceptions: the chief refrains from wielding ostentatious authority and strives to reflect in his deeds the consensus of the community, established through personal discussions with each of its members. Conversely, sheep-raising in the Mediterranean basin is characterized by direct positive action, since it entails permanent contact with the animal, which is entirely dependent on the shepherd for its survival. This directive attitude towards the flock manifests itself, in barely transposed guise, in Western political philosophy, wherein the figure of the Good Shepherd has passed since biblical times for an ideal incarnation of the sovereign. The treatment of nature and the treatment of others in these two cases reflect contrasting principles of behaviour towards living beings. Thus, between a structuralist nature that is good to think and a Marxist nature that is good to exploit there is perhaps room for a nature that is merely good to socialize.

The idea that there is a homology between the way in which people deal with nature and the way in which they treat each other may appear less powerfully 'explanatory' than the thesis that 'productive forces' are ultimately determinant, but it is also less constraining. It implies that there are correspondences between two fields of social practice without presuming causal links. However, if this idea is to be converted into a heuristic hypothesis, these correspondences must be both systematic and finite in number, and each must constitute an elementary principle in the construction of social practice.

The hypothesis gains strength from a demonstration that a relatively homogeneous class of societies objectifies nature according to entirely different patterns in globally similar ecosystems or, conversely, imposes globally similar modalities on entirely different ecosystems (which, in the extreme case, would suggest that ecological differences were irrelevant).

Marxist theory has long sought to identify specific types of social uses of nature. These are defined by characteristic modes of control of the means and results of material production. The same mode may develop in distinct ecological surroundings so long as they offer the minimum conditions required by the relevant productive forces. For instance, the relations of production typical of the

'Asiatic mode of production' have been identified in such ecologically distinct parts of the world as China, India, most of South-East Asia, Peru and Mexico, Western Africa, Mesopotamia, and Egypt (Centre d'Etudes et de Recherches Marxistes 1969). The various ecosystems of these areas had only one common characteristic: they could support highly productive forms of agriculture which could be enhanced by the introduction of complex systems of drainage, irrigation, and terracing.

Whereas Marxist theory does, therefore, provisionally order the very various historical social systems of production into coherent aggregates, it is incapable of explaining why many societies whose ecology and relations of production are similar nevertheless conceptualize their relationship to the environment in very different ways. The examples chosen by Haudricourt to illustrate his argument are hardly illuminating, since they can be reduced to a broad opposition between the Western world, dominated by systems of direct positive action, and the Far East (including Oceania), favouring indirect negative action. Both approaches ignore a basic objective of the anthropological research programme, taking no account of the cultural variability which exists within great regional areas where different peoples have the same environment, the same technology, and the same structure of production.

Amazonia offers a dramatic instance of a situation in which peoples who use a similar environment in an almost identical manner nevertheless objectify nature and society through very different schemes. Before I explore this case in more detail, however, a problem of definition remains to be resolved.

TOTEMIC SYSTEMS AND ANIMIC SYSTEMS

When analysing the treatment of 'nature' by pre-literate peoples the anthropologist faces a difficulty which is not purely semantic. Those peoples who, by an amusing irony, have long been described as 'natural' are in fact as far as possible from the concept of 'nature' we have inherited from Plato and Aristotle, since they usually endow the plants and animals of their environment with many of the characteristics of social life. The distinction between the treatment of nature and the treatment of human beings is thus purely analytical and almost never corresponds to the hierarchical ordering of life-forms made by cultures that do not make use of a dichotomy between nature and society. On the contrary, the 'savage mind' imposes a continuity between the social and natural domains by means of two processes. The first, admirably defined by Lévi-Strauss, is the logic of totemic classification. This makes use of empirically observable discontinuities between natural species to organize, conceptually, a segmentary order delimiting social units (Lévi-Strauss 1962b). Plants and animals offer natural stimuli to the taxonomic imagination. Their ethological and morphological discontinuities manifest contrasting qualities. Accordingly, they become signs which are particularly apt for expressing, in meta-phoric terms, the internal differences which inform the social order. This interpretation contradicts psychological, evolutionist, and utilitarian explanations of totemism, but it nevertheless leaves us with a considerable analytical residue, which might be termed, for the time being, 'animism'.

Among other things, animism is the belief that natural beings possess their own spiritual principles and that it is therefore poss-ible for humans to establish with these entities personal relations of a certain kind – relations of protection, seduction, hostility, alliance, or exchange of services. Modern anthropology has been extremely reticent on the topic of animism thus defined,[4] perhaps out of an implicit fear of drawing undue attention to an apparently irrational aspect of the life of archaic societies – an aspect that cannot easily be reduced to one of those universal operations of the mind which have been identified as the 'logic of the concrete' and which can be shown to operate in myths or taxonomies.

Nevertheless, animism can also be considered as a kind of social objectification of nature. It endows natural beings not only with human dispositions, granting them the status of persons with human emotions and often the ability to talk, but also with social attributes – a hierarchy of positions, behaviours based on kinship, respect for certain norms of conduct. In that sense, what I shall now term animic systems[5] are a *symmetrical inversion* of totemic classifications: they do not exploit the differential relations between natural species to confer a conceptual order on society but rather use the elementary categories structuring social life to organize, in conceptual terms, the relations between human beings and natural species. Animic systems do not treat plants and animals as mere signs or as privileged operators of taxonomic thought; they treat them as proper persons, as irreducible categories. The relation of plants and animals to humans is not metaphorical, as in totemism, but at the most, and then only in certain cases, metonymic. Despite the fact that they are splendid instances of what Mauss termed the 'total social phenomenon' (one of the very few original concepts ever produced by anthropology) and, as such, privileged indicators of our elusive schemes of praxis, animic systems are still largely unexplored. Identified with precision, they might help us to conceptualize a few of the principles which underpin the construction of the social order without doing violence to the diversity of reality or to the requirements of reason.

SOCIOLOGIES OF NATURE AND ECOLOGIES OF SOCIETY

The native Americas offer countless instances of animic systems and combinations of animic and totemic systems, a complex configuration very seldom found anywhere else. However, the methodological considerations specified in my introductory remarks make it preferable to compare animic systems in an area where there is little internal variation in ecology, technology, and systems of production. Amazonia unquestionably meets these requirements. From the slopes of the Andes to the mouth of the Amazon and from the Guyana shield to the northern Mato Grosso, the apparently uniform cover of the equatorial rain forest constitutes a generalized ecosystem characterized by a great diversity of vegetal and animal species but a small number of individuals per species.

There are notable local variations in the quality of the soils and in the availability of natural resources, particularly game and fish; but, as I have shown elsewhere (Descola 1986a), such variations have only a minor effect on the native modes of use of nature, which, most ethnographers agree, are relatively uniform throughout the area. Characteristically, Amazonian Indians are predators-gardeners who, in contrast to most other – notably Oceanian – tropical swidden horticulturalists, base their subsistence as much on hunting and fishing as on the cultivation of root crops (mainly manioc, domesticated in that part of the world at least 5,000 years ago). Despite this balanced combination of food procurement techniques, however, native Amazonian mythologies and cosmologies, magical techniques, and systems of values abundantly testify that the strategic focus of the objectification of nature is upon the wild fauna and its socialization. Contemporary native Amazonians also present striking similarities in social morphology: small, ideally self-sufficient, politically independent, and relatively egalitarian local groups, division of labour exclusively by sex and age, prevalence of cognatic systems, relations with the outside usually characterized by hostility, indifference to genea-logical continuities and ancestry. In the few societies where they exist, unilineal descent units do not function as corporate groups controlling access to material resources. Rather, they form the basis for the collective ownership of symbolic possessions (ornaments, songs, musical instruments, ritual prerogatives, etc.) the use of which is deemed necessary for the reproduction of society as a whole.

This apparent uniformity at the level of social practices as well as that of material and ideal relations with the environment is paired, however, with great variety in the schemes regulating the treatment of nature and of others. Basic to many Amazonian animic systems is a view of the universe as a gigantic closed circuit within which there is a constant circulation of the substances, souls, and iden-tities held to be necessary for the conservation of the world and the perpetuation of the social order. Since nature and society are not in this case separated by ontological boundaries, any death, whether of a human or of an animal, implies a break in the continuity of the flow of life. The temporarily disturbed equilibrium must then be immediately re-established by ritual operations such as endo- or exocannibalism, head-hunting, sexual abstinence, the propitiation of tutelary spirits, and food prohibitions. The means adopted by each culture to restore the state of homeostasis momentarily upset by the loss of a life differ widely according to the conceptions of the principles of identity and difference which govern the relations between human beings and between them and animals.

I will endeavour to analyse two Amazonian modalities of the social treatment of nature and of others, selecting for the purpose of demonstration processes of compensation which are meant to restore equilibrium following a death. These illustrate how antithetical schemes can structure the praxis of societies that are very close both culturally and geographically.

The first mechanism I will examine is based on a principle of strict equivalence between humans and animals. The human dead are recycled in a series of energetic exchanges with nature, filling the gaps in the animal populations which have been caused by hunting. The second mechanism is based on a deliberate negation of peaceful exchange, since the death of a human can only be compensated for by the violent capture of the vital strength, the identity, or the offspring of an individual alien to the local

group. Balance is restored in each case, but by two very different processes: in one instance by an act of reciprocity with
nature, which converts a human soul into a potential game animal,
and in the other by an act of predation which is metaphorically
homologous to hunting but entirely internal to the social sphere
(see Descola 1990).

The Desana of the north-western Amazon offer a striking illustration of the first of these schemes (Reichel-Dolmatoff 1971).
According to this tribe of the Tukano linguistic family, all energy
proceeds directly from Father Sun and ensures the vital continuity
of humans, animals, and plants through the cycle of fertilization,
gestation, and growth. The amount of energy produced by Father
Sun is finite, and it flows in an immense closed circuit which integrates the whole biosphere. To avoid 'entropic' loss, the exchanges
of energy between nature and society must be organized in such a
way as to allow for the reincorporation into the closed circuit of the
particles of energy captured by human beings (for instance, through
hunting). The main process of energetic feedback is based on the
circulation of human souls. After death, the souls of Desana usually
go to the subterranean or subaquatic homes of the deities ruling
game and fish. These are conceived of as enormous warehouses in
which all the animals of the forest and of the river are stored in good
order. The shaman of the local group regularly visits the Master of
Animals during a hallucinogenic trance induced by powerful vegetal
narcotics. There he negotiates with the deity for a certain number of
animals to be set free in the jungle, where they will be hunted by the
members of his local group. Each animal released for hunting must
be compensated for by the gift of the soul of a deceased human.
This soul will be transformed into an animal of the same species,
to be stored in the house of the Master of Animals. As reciprocal
substitutes, humans and animals thus enjoy equal status in the vast
community of living energy. Together they contribute to the general
equilibrium of energy flows, since their functions in this quest for
homeostasis are reversible.

The social organization of the Desana, like that of the other
Tukano tribes of the Vaupés area, is based on a principle of mutual
dependence that is strikingly similar to the one that organizes their
relations to the animal world. The physical and symbolic reproduction of each community is the product of the circulation of women
and of the distribution of ritual functions among a set of sixteen
tribes which all speak different languages (Jackson 1983). Each

patrilineal local group exchanges women with homologous exo-
gamic units belonging to different tribes, so that the perpetuation
of a community depends on a regular flow of women who speak
different languages from their husbands.

Apart from this linguistic exogamy, other factors contribute to
the structuring of the Tukano tribes as an integrated regional
system. First, the mythology postulates a common origin for all
the tribes and assigns to each a specific location and hierarchical
position according to its place and order of appearance. Second,
the ritual specialization of each group, entailing the participation of individuals from several tribes in the main ceremonies,
is oriented towards a celebration of the etiology of the totality
(S. Hugh-Jones 1979). Finally, the regional division of labour
attributes to each tribe a monopoly on the production of a certain
type of artefact (hammocks, canoes, manioc graters, etc.), thus
requiring the exchange of the products of their specialized crafts.
Despite linguistic diversity, each tribe, each local group, conceives
of itself as an element in a huge metasystem, owing its material and
symbolic continuity to regulated exchanges with the other parts
of the whole. As in the system of relationships with the animal
world, the Tukano social domain is entirely ruled by a logic of
reciprocity.

In societies in which the second scheme is dominant, in contrast,
the circulation of energies, substances, or identities excludes non-
human natural beings, so that the deficit generated by the death of
a human being must be compensated by a recycling process within
the human sphere, by means of cannibalism or head-hunting – two
phenomena which are entirely similar from this point of view (see
Lévi-Strauss 1984: 142). Among the Jivaro tribes of the Upper
Amazon, for example, the shrinking of an enemy's head fulfils
a double purpose. It neutralizes a principle of revenge (*emesak*),
emanating from the man just killed, by sealing it into the severed
head; and it deprives the victim of his original identity in order to
transfer it to the local group of the killer, where it will become the
principle of production of a child. By shrinking the head and using
it as an operator of transformation in the context of a lengthy and
complex ritual, the victorious warrior will protect himself from the
torments that the *emesak* might inflict on him. At the same time,
he will capture a virgin identity which will allow his kindred to
perpetuate itself without incurring the obligations of reciprocity
inherent in the marriage alliance (Taylor 1985, n.d.).

The enemies from among whom heads are taken must be neither too close sociologically nor too distant, since they are called upon to provide an identity that is culturally acceptable and yet perceived as different. A warrior therefore always takes a head from within the Jivaro linguistic group but from a tribe considered different from his own. This is all very remote from the law of compensation so meticulously observed by the Tukano groups. Head-hunting is a predatory process of accumulation which deliberately excludes reciprocity. However, the compensation for a head is always exacted forcefully in the long term, since the laws of revenge require that a killing never be left unpunished. The benefit brought by the taking of a head is always temporary, and the captured identity is later redistributed in an endless dialectic of violence.

Although no heads are taken during intratribal feuding, it involves a similar negation of reciprocity. Whatever the motives invoked for launching a feud between kindred-based groups, the killing of an enemy belonging to the same tribe very often entails the abduction of his wives and young children. The women are added to the spouses of the killer, while the children are adopted and socialized as kin (Descola 1986b). The abduction of women and children from among neighbouring local groups may never be a sufficient and explicit reason for engaging in a feud, but it is often an expected, even desired, result of its escalation. The benefit is twofold for the victorious warrior: he takes vengeance for a real or imaginary offence and he adds to his household while evading the obligations of affinity.

Evident both in intratribal feuding and in intertribal warfare, this remarkable negation of peaceful exchange finds its exact correspondence in the Jivaro ideology of hunting, which minimizes the symbolic compensation offered to game. Hunters address magical songs (*anent*) to the Mothers of Game and to the prototypes of each species (*amana*) in order to solicit their help in getting their prey. These songs express the idea that the hunter and his game are linked by a metaphorical relation of affinity. The game is called 'brother-in-law'. Hunting is represented as an act of collaboration between affines, and the final step – the actual killing of the animal – is veiled behind metaphors and playful euphemisms (Descola 1986a). By accounting his prey a relative and addressing friendly words to it, the hunter engages in a culturally specified deception that denies the unequal relationship which in reality exists between human beings and their animal victims. The objective is to allay the suspicions of these furry and feathery 'brothers-in-law' so that they will not avoid the hunter's darts or bear him a grudge because of his cannibalistic tendencies.

The contrast to the Desana cosmology is stark. There is absolutely no idea here of a general circulation of energy that would include natural objects. No compensation is given to the animals or to the Mothers of Game for the lives taken by the hunters. This matter-of-fact type of predation is only thinly disguised by the flimsy appearance of an affinal symbolism wherein one of the parties is an eternal donor while the other never respects the obligation to give back. The abduction of real or virtual identities among close or distant enemies and the incorporation of animals under cover of a fictive affinity thus express in different domains an identical negation of reciprocity in exchanges with others. But while humans are able to re-establish a balance through revenge, game must simply suffer the bad faith of these murderous 'brothers-in-law' who make their affines their preferred food.

Separated by only a few hundred kilometers, the tribes of the Tukano and Jivaro linguistic families live dispersed in small, independent local groups. They exploit, with notable efficiency, similar ecosystems, deploying similar technologies and organizing themselves by similar divisions of labour. Finally, they conceive their relations to the animal world in terms of the categories which structure social life, according to the logic characteristic of animic systems. Nevertheless, they hold quite different ideas about their relationships to nature and to others. The Tukano devote themselves to a punctilious reciprocity imposed by a social system and a cosmology animated by the constant circulation of bodies, souls, and objects between all levels of nature and society.[6] This huge metasystem is closed, and the conservation of its internal movement requires that its elements constantly shift their positions. By contrast, the Jivaro local groups seem obsessed by the idea of reproducing themselves à l'identique, and they poach from others the persons and identities they require. They deny compensation to game, through the subterfuge of a mock affinity, and also to the kin of their victims, who have to snatch it away from them by taking their lives. Their treatment of nature and treatment of others is governed by an ideology of predation, which is the negation of exchange.

The existence of these two antithetical schemes among Tukano and Jivaro does not mean that all Amerindian animic systems could be placed within the framework of an elementary opposition between exchange and predation. In other South American native societies, sociologically and ecologically very close to those we have examined, very different formulae may characterize the modes of treatment of nature and of others. A very brief example will allow me to illustrate this point.

The Arawak tribes who live in the Amazonian foothills of the central Peruvian Andes have been exposed since long before the Spanish conquest to constant attempts at invasion and annexation, first by Andean chiefdoms and states, then by the Spaniards, and finally by post-colonial Peruvians. Except for brief periods of very localized colonial domination, these attempts were successfully repelled until the beginning of this century.

The cosmologies of these tribes are all organized according to a dualist principle which distributes human societies, animals, and supernatural beings in two domains, ontologically distinct and mutually antagonistic (Weiss 1969, Renard-Casevitz 1985). One of these domains has a positive value and includes beings that share an essence: the Arawak tribes and some of their jungle Indian neighbours with whom marriage alliance is possible, the empyrean divinities, the supernatural masters of game, and most of the game itself, particularly the birds. Hunting is accordingly conceived as a brief metempsychosis during which the animals willingly offer to humans their corporeal outer cover while retaining their souls, which are immediately reincarnated in other bodies. The second domain has a negative value and is defined by its radical otherness. It includes all the humans of the Andes, be they Indians or whites (including Tupac Amaru guerrillas), and bewitching animals and their masters, the evil spirits. The relation between the two domains is one of a struggle between good and evil, continuing through the centuries and finding expression in real or magical warfare.

In contradistinction to the preceding examples, the Arawak cosmologies offer a division of the world into two fields, both combining natural and social elements but opposed in Manichean fashion. Unlike other dualist systems that are animated by an internal dialectic, these involve no processes of exchange or predation, and no principle of a transfer of energies or identities.

CONCLUSION

Can these localized ethnological enquiries contribute in any way to the vast anthropological programme sketched in the introduction? I have briefly analysed the modes of treatment of nature and of others specific to native Amazonian societies belonging to three great cultural and linguistic families which have been clearly differentiated by the ethnographic literature. There is little to distinguish these societies from the point of view of what Julian Steward terms their 'cultural core' or at the level of 'productive forces' (in the Marxist sense) or symbolic logics (animic systems). The cultural variations they display, conveyed by immediately recognizable distinctive styles, seem to arise from three contrasted formulae that may provisionally be termed exchange, predation, and ontological dualism.

At the present level of analysis, the exact terms used to denote these systems of relations are of little consequence. One might just as well express them in the language of kinship analysis (generalized exchange for the Tukano, involuntary restricted exchange for the Jivaro, dualist organization with endogamous moieties for the Arawak) or even in the terms applied in the structural analysis of myths (for Tukano, givers of identities are to receivers of identity as humans are to animals, and reciprocally; for Jivaro, falsely different predators of identities are to really identical purveyors of identities as humans really different from animals are to animals falsely identified with humans; for Arawak, one kind of human is to a kind of humans and animals as one kind of animal is to a kind of animals and humans).

These formulae are accessible analytically through the study of the modes of representation of relations to nature, but they are never explicitly defined by native exegesis. They may be culture-specific, but unrelated societies in the same geographical area present similar structuring principles while others seem to be governed by entirely different formulae. Moreover, the ways in which the possible modes of treatment of nature and of others might be combined cannot be so great as to permit a specific formula for each known culture. It is more likely that these formulae express underlying schemes that inform the rules by which social practice is constructed, organizing at once political conceptions and representations of social relations, structures of exchange and ideological productions. Their effect is to generate a configuration of cultural traits specific to a society from the point of view of an outside observer and experienced as normative by the people under study.

Are we, then, to consider these schemes as pure products of the human mind? Even though their logic probably takes as its elementary units sets of objects that are shaped by universal modes of recognition and classification of living beings, it would be a daring leap to treat them as cognitive universals. On the other hand, it is reasonable to see them as local expressions of cultural invariants, synthesizing in a finite number of mental structures certain properties of social life as they are objectified in relation to nature.

Perhaps because it has been too often confused with the quest for human universals, the search for cultural invariants has gone out of fashion, especially in the Anglo-Saxon world. However, it remains a promising endeavour. A recent illustration of its value can be found in the work of Françoise Héritier-Augé, who explains the logic of kinship terminologies in terms of the combination of three universal rules, themselves grounded in biological differences (Héritier-Augé 1981). Though they are obviously less formalized than kinship terminologies, modes of representation of relations to nature present certain similar characteristics: a substratum organized on the basis of natural discontinuities, and modes of relations that combine elementary units such as sexual differentiation, classes of life-forms, categories of tools and operations, types of substances and physiological processes, forms of exchange, and systems of energy flows. These configurations are ecological in the strict sense of the term, since they represent a specific patterning of interaction between mind and matter. As such, they are much more susceptible to change than are kinship terminologies, for their material determinants are more numerous and more complex: the modification of only some elements may precipitate the establishment of a new combination. This feature may help to explain the differential rate of transformation of societies. Some will retain their basic schemes of praxis much longer than others, even if their social, economic, and political organizations undergo important mutations, provided that these transformations do not render obsolete the elementary modes of relations which constitute the components of the scheme.

It should be clear by now that, for me, the subject of anthropology cannot be 'society', a mere empirical datum with no real boundaries beyond those that stem from the subjective vantage point assumed by the observer, whether this is imposed or elected. This does not mean that individual societies do not exist but only that they are not autonomously defined and substantive realities which can be inventoried and compared. In short, and to draw a metaphor from the natural sciences, rather than the Linnaean classifications of perceptually evident entities I favour the Haeckelian approach, which studies localized systems of interrelations. That the extent of such systems often corresponds to the empirical boundaries of an actual society implies not that the society is a closed totality but that it represents the visible product of the operation of the system.

Each localized system of interrelations exhibits a specific combination of elementary components which can probably be ascribed to a limited repertory of cultural invariants. More than the Darwinian ecology of Haeckel and his successors, anthropology requires a genuine symbolic ecology. In different guises this project has been attempted by anthropologists from Frazer to Bateson. Its achievement is probably now within our reach.

NOTES

1 The main ideas presented here were developed in the course of my weekly seminar at the Ecole des Hautes Etudes en Sciences Sociales; before discussing them at the EASA meeting in Coimbra, I was given a challenging opportunity to rework some of their formulations as a result of two lectures given at the Universities of Bergen and Oslo. I am very grateful to Claude Lévi-Strauss and Ann-Christine Taylor for their insightful comments on an earlier draft of the paper, and to the latter and Adam Kuper for their invaluable linguistic assistance.

2 As Maurice Godelier pithily expresses it, 'man has a history because he transforms nature' (1984: 10, my translation).

3 As in the famous and often quoted sentence from *The Poverty of Philosophy*: 'The hand-mill will give you the society with the suzerain; the steam-mill, the society with the industrial capitalist' (Marx 1965 [1847]: 79, my translation).

4 My definition of animism is deliberately restrictive with respect to the Tylorian conception: it corresponds to certain types of relations between nature and society, usually called 'individual totemism' in the anthropological literature, which associate a single person either with a natural category or with an individual plant or animal (see Lévi-Strauss 1982b: 23–5). Conversely, totemic classifications express a relation between a social group and a natural category (ibid.). Animism can be considered as an analytical residue of totemism only in the strict sense of each term as defined here and in the light of Lévi-Strauss's

breakthrough in *Le totémisme aujourd'hui* (1962b). Historically, on the other hand, as Lévi-Strauss himself has pointed out, the analysis of totemism was confined to certain modalities within the wider domain of 'classical' animism.

5 Although reluctant to coin neologisms, I prefer 'animic' to 'animist', the latter being too closely associated with an outdated or pejorative conception of primitive religion.

6 Reciprocity does not preclude internal violence, provided the latter appears either as a kind of *acte gratuit* or as a form of communication or spatial integration. We have little information on Tukano warfare, which ceased a long time ago. We do know, however, that a clear-cut distinction was made between wife-raiding and killing proper. Wife-raiding between semi-distant Tukano tribes was common, generally bloodless, explicitly linked to hunting, and considered a 'natural' and alternative version of the usual marriage exchange (C. Hugh-Jones 1979: 223; see also Århem 1981: 160). The killing of a man in a distant and totally unrelated tribe was a much more drastic form of violence, since it implied the reduction of another group's procreative power and, consequently, an entropic loss affecting the whole metasystem. Unlike Jivaro head-hunting, this 'gratuitous' destruction was not a process of predation, since it entailed no gain of energy or generative capacity for the killer's group. It is not surprising, then, that the figure of the warrior (*masa sīari masa*, 'people-killing people') was considered as an extreme negative embodiment of intra-Tukano interaction (C. Hugh-Jones 1979: 64).

REFERENCES

Århem, K. (1981) *Makuna Social Organization: A Study in Descent, Alliance, and the Formation of Corporate Groups in the North-Western Amazon*, Uppsala: Acta Universitatis Upsaliensis.

Berlin, B., Breedlove, D. and Raven, P. (1973) 'General principles of classification and nomenclature in folk biology', *American Anthropologist* 75: 214–42.

Centre d'Etudes et de Recherches Marxistes (1969) *Sur le 'mode de production asiatique'*, Paris: Editions Sociales.

Descola P. H. (1986a) *La nature domestique: Symbolisme et praxis dans l'écologie des Achuar*, Paris: Fondation Singer-Polignac/Editions de la Maison des Sciences de l'Homme.

——(1986b) 'Contrôle social de la transgression et guerre de vendetta dans le Haut Amazone', *Droit et Cultures* 11: 137–40.

——(1990) 'Cosmologies du chasseur amazonien', in S. Devers (ed.) *Pour Jean Malaurie*, Paris: Plon.

Godelier, M. (1984) *L'idéel et le matériel: Pensée, économies, sociétés*, Paris: Fayard.

Haudricourt, G. A. (1962) 'Domestication des animaux, culture des plantes et traitement d'autrui', *L'Homme* 2, 1: 40–50.

Héritier-Augé, F. (1981) *L'exercice de la parenté*, Paris: Hautes Etudes, Gallimard–Le Seuil.

Hugh-Jones, C. (1979) *From the Milk River: Spatial and Temporal Processes in Northwest Amazonia*, Cambridge: Cambridge University Press.

Hugh-Jones, S. (1979) *The Palm and the Pleiades: Initiation and Cosmology in Northwest Amazonia*, Cambridge: Cambridge University Press.

Jackson, J. (1983) *The Fish People: Linguistic Exogamy and Tukanoan Identity in the Northwest Amazon*, Cambridge: Cambridge University Press.

Lévi-Strauss, C. (1962a) *La pensée sauvage*, Paris: Plon.

——(1962b) *Le totémisme aujourd'hui*, Paris: Plon.

——(1984) *Paroles données*, Paris: Plon.

Marx, K. (1965) *Oeuvres*. Vol. 1. *Economie*, ed. M. Rubel, Paris: Bibliothèque de la Pléiade.

Reichel-Dolmatoff, G. (1971) *Amazonian Cosmos: The Sexual and Religious Symbolism of the Tukano Indians*, Chicago and London: University of Chicago Press.

Renard-Casevitz, F. M. (1985) 'Guerre, violence et identité à partir des sociétés du piémont amazonien des Andes centrales', *Cahiers ORSTOM* (série Sciences Humaines) 21, 1: 81–98.

Sperber, D. (1982) 'Apparently irrational beliefs', in M. Hollis and S. Lukes (eds) *Rationality and Relativism*, Oxford: Blackwell.

Taylor, A. C. (1985) 'L'art de la réduction: La guerre et les mécanismes de la différenciation tribale dans la culture jivaro', *Journal de la Société des Américanistes* 71: 159–73.

——(n.d.) 'Les bons ennemis et les mauvais parents: Le traitement symbolique de l'alliance dans les rituels shuar de chasse aux têtes', in E. Copet-Rougier and F. Héritier-Augé (eds) *La symbolique de l'alliance*, Paris: Editions des Archives Contemporaines.

Weiss, G. (1969) *The Cosmology of the Campa Indians of Eastern Peru*, Ann Arbor: Xerox University Microfilms.

Chapter 6

What goes without saying
The conceptualization of Zafimaniry society

Maurice Bloch

A problem which lurks uneasily in the prefaces of most anthropological monographs and worries, or should worry, all fieldworking
anthropologists is that the way anthropologists conceptualize the
societies they have studied in their ethnographic accounts almost
always seems alien, bizarre, or impossibly complicated to the
people of those societies. Perhaps this would not matter if ethnographies claimed only to be description from the outside; however,
most accounts attempt, at least in part, to represent a society and
ways of thinking about it from the insiders' point of view. Perhaps,
then, we could get rid of the difficulty by saying that this disturbing
lack of recognition was just a problem of vocabulary; after all,
most people in most parts of the world are unacquainted with the
technical terms and literary conventions of academic anthropology.
But one has to face the fact that, if this were all there was to it,
anyone who was reasonably good at paraphrase would surely be
able to cross the communication gap and produce a non-technically
worded ethnography with which informants would largely agree.
Clearly, this is not often the case. The problem of lack of validation
by the people with whom anthropologists work begins, then, to
look like a very serious one.

In fact, the basis of the problem lies in something much more
damaging than is normally recognized. Anthropological accounts,
I believe, work from a false theory of cognition. As a result, when
they attempt to represent the way the people studied conceptualize
their society, they do so in terms which do not match the way *any*
human beings conceptualize *anything* fundamental and familiar in
any society or culture. In imagining how the people they study

conceptualize society anthropologists use the common folk view of thought current in both Western and many other societies. But there is considerable evidence that this folk theory is as wrong about psychological processes as the folk theory of physics is wrong about the nature of energy (see Bechtel 1990; Churchland and Sejnowski 1989).

The folk model, which is also widely assumed in Western philosophy, is that thought is logic-sentential and language-like. We tend to imagine thinking as a kind of silent soliloquizing wherein the building blocks are words with their definitions and the process itself involves linking propositions by logical inferences in a single lineal sequence. By contrast, much recent work in cognitive science strongly suggests that everyday thought is not 'language-like', that it does not involve linking propositions in a single sequence in the way language represents reasoning. Rather, it relies on clumped networks of signification which *require* that they be organized in ways which are not lineal but multi-stranded if they are to be used at the amazing speed necessary to draw on complex stored information in everyday activity. If that is so, anthropologists are presented with two problems.

The first is that the people we study are unlikely to be able easily to describe their thought processes for anthropologists through what they say, since language is an inappropriate medium for evoking the non-lineal organization of everyday cognition. (This, like several other points I make in this chapter, was pointed out in a different way by Bourdieu in 1972.) Furthermore, since having to explain to others what one thinks through an inappropriate medium, viz., language, is a familiar problem in all cultures, informants asked to give retrospective accounts of their thought processes – a common enough occurrence in normal life – are able to fall back on the conventions by which the problem is normally avoided. These conventions of everyday discourse usually involve reinventing a hypothetical quasi-linguistic lineal, rational thought process which appears to lead satisfactorily to the conclusions reached. But it does so deceptively in terms of the way we, and they, think we think because it follows the folk theory of thought shared by the anthropologist and the informant. In other words, the problem of explaining to others how we reach a decision is solved by what we would normally call *post hoc* rationalizations, and these are what anthropologists are given when they too ask for retrospective explanations of actions.

The second problem which arises from the impossibility of matching the organization of everyday thought to the semantics of natural language relates to the anthropologists' own accounts of their informants' thought processes. Anthropologists write books, in which information is inevitably presented by means of language, and so their medium makes them slip far too easily into representing the hypothesized thought processes of those they study as though these also inevitably assumed the organizational logic of the semantics of language. Furthermore, the problem is not just one of medium; anthropologists naturally attempt to produce accounts of intellectual processes which will prove persuasive to their readers, and readers, along with the anthropologists' informants, expect accounts of the thought of the people studied to match the folk theory of thought. As a result, a kind of double complicity is all too easily established between anthropologists and their readers and between anthropologists and their informants – a double complicity which leads to representations of thought in logic-sentential terms.

But in fact, although a plausible account is thereby produced, it leaves all the main participants uncomfortable. Informants feel that anthropologists' accounts are not right. Readers are also suspicious of accounts of the culture of others which, although plausible, are quite unlike the way they experience their own culture. Anthropologists themselves are worried by the fact that the acceptable ethnographies they produce with such effort have somehow lost 'what it was really like'. This is something which they sometimes wrongly attribute to the difficulty of rendering one text into another, while what they should be thinking about is the problem of rendering into a text something which is not a text.

Fortunately, as suggested above, recent work in cognitive science helps us resist the insidious influence of the folk theory of thought by suggesting an alternative to it. This work, although still tentative, provides scientific ammunition against the logic-sentential folk model of thought implied by language and suggests another way in which thought is organized which, furthermore, is intuitively attractive to a field-working anthropologist. This is so because, while the *post hoc* overlinguistic rationalizations of most ethnography seem distant from what one feels is going on in real situations in the field, the newer theory of thought intuitively seems to correspond to the way informants actually operate in everyday situations.

It is impossible to discuss fully here the theoretical basis of this alternative view of cognition (but see Churchland and Sejnowski 1989; Bloch 1991). The core of the approach, usually known as connectionism, is the idea that most knowledge, especially the knowledge involved in everyday practice, does not take a linear, logic-sentential form but rather is organized into highly complex and integrated networks or mental models most elements of which are connected to each other in a great variety of ways. The models form conceptual clumps which are not language-like precisely because of the simultaneous multiplicity of ways in which information is integrated in them. These mental models are, what is more, only partly linguistic; they also integrate visual imagery, other sensory cognition, the cognitive aspects of learned practices, evaluations, memories of sensations, and memories of typical examples. Not only are these mental models not lineal in their internal organization but information from them can be accessed simultaneously from many different parts of the model through 'multiple parallel processing'. This is what enables people to cope with information as rapidly as they, and probably other animals, do in normal, everyday situations.

There is, of course, no question of anthropologists' studying these mental models directly in any detail. However, the awareness that cultural knowledge is likely to be organized in this way should modify the way in which we represent actors' ways of thinking in general and their conceptualizations of society in particular. It should make anthropologists suspicious of overlinguistic, over-logic-sentential conceptualizations and prompt them to search for alternatives which could correspond to the clumped models just discussed. Furthermore, in going in this direction I believe we will find that much of the often-expressed discomfort with ethnography may disappear and that the problem that the people we study cannot relate to our accounts of them may be diminished.

This paper is an attempt to go some way towards writing ethnography in such a way that actors' concepts of society are represented not as strings of terms and propositions but as governed by lived-in models, that is, models based as much in experience, practice, sight, and sensation as in language. In trying to do this there can be no avoiding the problem that inevitably this information is presented in a medium, language, whose semantic organization leads back to the kind of presentation from which I am trying to escape, but it is also true that language can be used, if not without difficulty, to talk about processes and patterns which are not in any way language-like. We should not mistake our account for what it refers to.

There is also another difficulty. Normally anthropologists who are trying to persuade their audience that what they are saying is a fair account of the concepts of the people they study tend to fall back on quoting their informants. This apparently innocent procedure is, however, for the reasons just discussed, potentially misleading, since people's explanations probably involve *post hoc* rationalizations of either a conventional or an innovative character. So, although I do use what people say in attempting to convey these mental models, these statements are merely purpose-specific periphery to the foundations of conceptualization. But then where do my data come from, and how can I persuade my readers of their relevance? Here I propose an awkward solution.

Through intimate participant observation over long periods of time, anthropologists learn how to live in a relatively coordinated way with their informants. In order to do this they must learn and internalize a great deal of the knowledge that the people they study must themselves have learnt and internalized. Now, if indeed anthropologists have learnt these clumped non-logic-sentential mental models which organize the cultures they study, they should be able to make at least plausible assertions of how their informants conceptualize the world as a result of their own introspection. I believe that readers who are convinced that anthropologists have carried out the kind of fieldwork necessary for this kind of understanding should be willing to give them the benefit of the doubt. This may seem to be asking a lot; in fact it does not call for more intellectual generosity than is normally required from the readers of academic texts, and sometimes perhaps not for such good reasons. Anthropologists' accounts of the thought processes of their informants accompanied by many verbatim statements, which therefore superficially appear based on irrefutable evidence, will on examination turn out to require almost as much trust from the reader because of the arbitrary way in which these statements must be selected. Furthermore, such language-based accounts are likely to be misleading because the style of presentation will inevitably suggest that the core of the actors' conceptualizations is these few selected verbal statements.

In this paper I shall therefore try to give, for the sake of demonstration, an ethnographic account of the conceptualization of society by a small group of people I studied in Madagascar called the Zafimaniry.[1] My description relies on the evocation of a few linked central mental models[2] which I believe are, when put together, sufficient to organize their conceptualization and practice of society. These models, as connectionist theories would lead us to expect, are not principally propositional in the traditional sense of the term, though they can be accessed in part through language, but partly visual, partly sensual, partly linked to performance. They are all anchored in practice and material experience, and this is what makes them 'obvious' to anybody, anthropologist or informant, who participates in Zafimaniry life. For this reason, my account would not, I am sure, appear in any way strange to my informants. Indeed, their reaction is that since what I am talking about is merely about what things 'are like' – people, trees, sex, gender, houses, and so on – it is a waste of time to talk much about them.[3]

In doing this I am implicitly criticizing some aspects of my earlier attempt at giving an account of their society (Bloch 1975). This article dealt with many other topics than the Zafimaniry's conceptualization of their society, and by these I stand. I tried to give an account of their social organization, especially their kinship organization, largely in terms of a fairly hazy moiety organization, complex marriage and filiation rules, and kinship terminology. After subsequent fieldwork I now find this attempt, although on the whole acceptable in terms of the facts it presented, to suffer precisely from giving the impression that the Zafimaniry's conceptualization of society could be given in the logic-sentential form criticized above, though this is precisely how social anthropologists traditionally proceed.[4]

The Zafimaniry are a group of shifting cultivators numbering about 20,000 who live in the eastern forest of Madagascar. Although they have in the past been incorporated into various states and kingdoms, they have, by and large, maintained a remarkable degree of autonomy up to the present day, and in most matters their villages, varying in size between 300 and 3,000 inhabitants, are practically self-governing. Here I attempt to give an account of how they conceptualize their society in terms of five linked mental models from which all the main principles of their social organization seem to flow: (1) the mental model of what people are like and how they mature, (2) the mental model of the differences and similarities between women and men, (3) the mental model of what a good marriage is like, (4) the mental model of what trees and wood are like, and (5) the mental model of what houses are like. These are all very simple models which misleadingly appear to the participants as merely emanations of the empirical, but when they are put together they produce the highly specific conceptualization of society which characterizes the Zafimaniry's view.

WHAT PEOPLE ARE LIKE AND HOW THEY MATURE

The Zafimaniry conceptualization of the maturation of the body focuses not so much on growth as on hardening and straightening. Thus Zafimaniry often play with the soft bodies of their babies and laugh over their bendability, calling the children, in an amused fashion, by the common Malagasy term for babies, which literally means 'water children'. In a similar mood they show each other the baby's fontanelle and the watery substance it covers. The change from bendable wetness to straight hardness is rarely commented upon in discourse, but its importance can be guessed at from continual allusions to the straight leg and arm bones of elders and ancestors and from the fact that people talk of the elders' 'straightening' the young as they show them the proper ways of behaving according to ancestral rules. Less direct is the way people expect to break their leg and arm bones more and more easily as they get old because, they sometimes say, the bones are 'harder'. Equally suggestive is the way people note and sometimes comment on the drying out of the skin of the old in relation to that of the young. All these cognitions, practices, and chance or more formal remarks indicate a general understanding of the maturing body which is unproblematically communicated without the anthropologist's necessarily being aware of the exact manner of this transmission.

This physical change in the body accompanies psychological development. Babies cannot talk and cannot be expected to do much for themselves. They do not exercise any moral judgement. This amoral unpredictability continues through youth and in some ways increases as the children get bigger and cause more chaos. Their behaviour soon becomes tinged with boisterous and unstable sexuality, and the boys tend to become aggressive. But a change occurs for both boys and girls at marriage. Marriage calms people down; their minds turn to practical matters to do with making their marriage successful, in particular rearing and being able to support children who themselves produce children, and so on. Later the psychological state typical of the married person is, and should be, gradually replaced by the *gravitas* of elders. Elders are calm, very stable people whose psychological disposition is the exact opposite of the playful quarrelsomeness of the young in that they are peacemakers who value unity and morality above all things.

This general process of psychological development is often commented upon and even explained by the Zafimaniry, but it is not the basis of the model any more than statements are the basis of the cognition of bodily development. The basis is the demonstrated and observed behaviour of people of different ages, together with the disapproval or surprise expressed when people display psychological behaviour inappropriate for their ages.

The model of maturation also has an aspect which concerns occupation. When the young are old enough to get about, they soon become little foragers. At first this happens in the village, and then, little by little, their activities take place ever farther away, sometimes deep in the forest, involving ever bigger finds and game. The children start with berries and insects, then move on to small fish and crustacea and then to birds and larger mammals. This period of foraging ends with marriage, but because boys marry later than girls (since girls mature earlier) the foraging stage continues longer and develops towards an extreme for young men when their hunting becomes associated with larger animals such as wild boar. This last stage of the foraging period also involves wage labouring; this consists exclusively of forestry work, which is easily assimilated to hunting and foraging both because it takes place deep in the forest and because the young male workers behave as if they were on a hunting trip, with boisterous mock aggression and the singing of hunting songs.

The foraging of the young is for the Zafimaniry an adventurous but not a serious form of activity; they say and demonstrate by their actions that it is a form of play. Consequently the product of such activity, although it is very important nutritionally and economically, is not, nor in their evaluation should it be, taken seriously. For example, when little girls sold some delicious forest fruit at a market for quite a lot of money, everybody commented that this was ridiculous. With marriage, the foraging of the young gives way to agriculture, which is and is recognized to be the typical activity of the married middle-aged. Unlike foraging, this is a serious business, and it is closely associated with the need to support children and grandchildren. Finally, middle age, dominated by agriculture and marriage, is gradually replaced by elderhood. In elderhood other types of activities dominate. At first carpentry and the carving of the wood which will strengthen and beautify the house become central activities for the relatively young male elder. Then, for both genders, various forms of highly valued oral activities come to the fore. These include making formal speeches, amongst them requests or thanks to the ancestors, speeches involved with formal visiting, church addresses, and above all the oratory of dispute settlement.

Maturation is therefore not just a matter of physical and psychological development but also a matter of changing occupation. This totality can be more completely grasped by briefly looking at two further facets of the model: language and locality.

The language of the young is and is often noted to be a tumble of rushed, often unfinished sentences. Their conversational style is marked by continual interruptions and what Karl Reisman called 'contrapuntal conversation' (Reisman 1974). In many ways it too is an aspect of play. The language of the middle-aged also relates to the character of the activities which dominate their lives. It is typically earnest conversation in which the different speakers do not interrupt each other and in which the intention of conveying information and of negotiation seems to govern the style of intercourse. Finally, the speech typical of elders is highly formalized, highly decorated, and largely formulaic in that it follows predictable models for thanks, greetings, prayers, etc. The manner of speaking is quiet and as if not addressed to anybody; it seems beyond dialogue. However, in contrast with the styles of conversation typical of the young and the middle-aged, the style of elders is employed only when they are *being* elders; the rest of the time they speak like middle-aged people.

Finally, there is a spatial aspect to all this. The young are always running about, as soon as they can they go off in search of forest products and adventure. The middle-aged also move about a lot, but they are ever more anchored to the house of their marriage. This stabilization and localization increase still further with the elders, who, as we shall see, gradually merge with the house itself.

THE DIFFERENCES AND SIMILARITIES BETWEEN WOMEN AND MEN

Gender is not for the Zafimaniry the prime identity that it may be in some cultures. First one is a child, an adult, an elder, a parent, etc., and *then* one is a special kind of child, a special kind of parent, etc., that is female or male. Furthermore, the relative prominence of gender differentiation varies with age. Gender becomes more important at adolescence and then becomes gradually less so.

However, women and men have certain bodily characteristics which mean that they are different. These bodily differences concern the linked activities of sex and the production of children. Because sex and reproduction require both women and men, these differences are complementary and not a matter of more or less. At the same time, there is a hierarchical aspect to gender. Insofar as they are comparable, women are usually physically weaker and, in a way which appears to the Zafimaniry inevitably linked, probably also mentally inferior to men, although in certain circumstances (which although unusual are not rare) it is possible for women to be intellectually superior and stronger than men. This is so, for example, if a wife fulfils her duties while a husband does not or if the man is weakened by disease or other infirmity or simply if she is big and he is small.

WHAT A GOOD MARRIAGE IS LIKE

The model of the good marriage is as central to Zafimaniry conceptualization as that concerning the maturation of people. The core of the model is the image of a complementary, loving, fruitful union of two spouses engaged in joint domestic and agricultural tasks.[5]

Fruitfulness manifests itself first of all in the number of children produced and then in the number of children produced by these children, and so on. Again, it is manifested in the success, principally the agricultural success, of the parents in providing for these children, grandchildren, and so on, so that they thrive. A fruitful marriage is one in which the combination of the spouses leads to the growth of a unity which they have created. This means that the children of the marriage are the continuation of this unity, and therefore siblings are part of a single totality since they are the outgrowth of the original unity produced by loving complementarity.

The centrality and character of this image of loving complementarity can be conveyed by a few hints provided by Zafimaniry ethnography. One of these is that parents who arrange that their children should marry keep this a secret from them. It is felt that parents can only point their children in the right direction, and mutual compatibility can only be achieved if it is believed by the parties to be spontaneous. Another hint is the fact that Zafimaniry diviners, in contrast to those in other parts of Madagascar, normally find the cause of sterility to be not a problem the woman has but the lack of compatibility of the pair. Then there is the total absence of public quarreling between spouses in a society where nothing much can be kept private and the fact that people say that if such quarreling became public the marriage would immediately break up.

At the heart of the model is the image of the couple cooperating harmoniously in the performance of single domestic and agricultural activities through different but complementary tasks. Most agricultural tasks are indeed carried out by husband-and-wife pairs working together, and this is often commented upon favourably. People often pointed out to me the emblematic significance of the particularly heavy work involved in carrying crops from the field to the house; this is a task that spouses share, although their ways of carrying, one on the head the other on the shoulder, are different.

Marital harmony is the product of the psychological and physiological compatibility of the spouses, but for the Zafimaniry this requires that a *balance* be established between the two parties. If the family of either the groom or the bride is much weaker, there cannot be a proper marriage, because a proper marriage requires that equal respect be paid to the origin of both spouses. Sexual unions in which this is not the case often occur, but to the Zafimaniry they are not marriages because marriage is marked by mutuality and reciprocal exchange at all levels. Balance is always threatened by the difficult intrusion of an element of imbalance brought about by the superiority of the man over the woman. Much of the Zafimaniry conceptualization of society flows from the attempt to reintroduce in this situation the balance of the good marriage.

A Zafimaniry marriage is the result of the stabilization of what starts as a playful, fleeting relationship between two very young persons who are like that because of their state of maturation. As the children grow up and form couples who begin to have regular sexual relationships, this fact becomes noticed, and the young people are forced to appear before the girl's parents in a simple ritual which is called *tapa maso* (literally, 'the breaking of the eyes'). This refers to the fact that it is very wrong for people of different generations, especially if they are of different sexes, to have knowledge of each other's sexual activity. The appearance of the young couple together asking for the girl's father's blessing therefore breaks this avoidance – it 'breaks the father's eyes'.

After the *tapa maso* the couple will most probably stay with the girl's parents until the next ritual, which is called the *fanambarana* (literally, 'the making clear'). The essential element of this ritual is the groom's fetching of the bride and her trousseau of kitchen furniture to his family's locality. The reason it is the bride who follows the groom and not the other way round is that the man is stronger than the woman. This fact, however, contradicts the image of balance, and so various strategies are adopted to restore it.

First of all, attempts are made during the *fanambarana* to produce a downright denial that an imbalance exists. The marriage is said to be a swop; everybody repeats the well-worn phrase that the marriage is 'an exchange of a male child for a female child', implying that the parents of the boy gain a daughter and the parents of the girl gain a son – and, indeed, from then on the spouses address their parents-in-law with the same terms as they use for their own parents. Similarly, people say that a marriage is 'the exchange of male orange for a female orange'. This gnomic statement is then explained as meaning that it is an exchange of like for like, since no one can tell the difference between the two sorts of oranges.

Other ways of lessening imbalance concern specific practices. The spouses must spend much time with the girl's parents, and they will seek the blessings of both sides equally for any important task. Their children are considered to be equally the grandchildren of both sides. Imbalance is also temporarily corrected by the fact that the obligations of the couple to the girl's parents have priority over their obligations to the boy's parents because, as they say, 'they are less often with the former'. Most important, the imbalance caused by gender is corrected by the introduction of the concept of the unity of siblings. This comes into play in two ways.

Since siblings are part of a unity, marriage to a particular person implies, to an extent, marriage to his or her siblings, including those of the other gender. The siblings of ego's spouse are also ego's spouses. Thus Zafimaniry men refer to the brothers of their wives and the husbands of their sisters by a term (*vady lahy*) which literally means 'male spouse', and Zafimaniry women refer to the sisters of their husbands and the wives of their brothers by a term (*vady vavy*) which literally means 'female spouse'. By stressing these 'marriage' relationships and the reciprocal and equal cooperation which exists between 'female spouses' and especially between 'male spouses', the marriage relationship regains a gender-free balance which the difference between women and men threatens to disrupt.

The unity of siblings is also used to recover the balance essential for the good marriage in an even more radical way. This involves making a specific marriage part of a reciprocal exchange wherein pairs of cross-sex young people classed as siblings by the kinship terminology intermarry simultaneously. Zafimaniry have a strong preference for marriage of a brother and a sister to sister and brother. This creates a pattern very similar to that familiar to anthropologists as cross-cousin marriage, and it has similar sociological effects in that it leads to a loose moiety system, something I discussed in a previous publication on the Zafimaniry (Bloch 1975). That this is so should not, however, make us forget that this moiety system is conceptualized as the result of the need for balance in a good marriage, not in the traditional description by means of rules and terminology which characterized my earlier attempt.

WHAT TREES AND WOOD ARE LIKE

The importance of trees and wood, two words which are translated into Malagasy by the single word *hazo*, is central to the Zafimaniry. As shifting cultivators they depend on burning wood to make fields; because the climate is so cold and damp they must have wood fires continually burning in their houses. Besides this they used to, and to a certain extent still do, make their cloth from the bark of trees, and their houses and most of their utensils are made of wood. It is not surprising, therefore, that all Zafimaniry possess very extensive scientific knowledge about wood, about the many species of trees, about the many different qualities of the woods they yield, and about the way different woods must be treated to prepare them for the various uses to which they are put.

The most valued trees and also the rarer ones are those which produce the kind of wood used in house building, and these must contain what the Zafimaniry call *teza*. The *teza* of trees is a dark impacted core which is much harder than the outer part, called by a term which normally refers to white of egg. It is often compared to the bones of animals and humans, which can also be called by the same word. A central image of *teza* is that it is what remains after a swidden has been fired, since this hardened core does not normally burn. Indeed, the word *teza* is the root of the verb *mateza*, 'to last or to remain'.

The maturation of trees with *teza* is of the greatest significance to the Zafimaniry. Young trees have no *teza* at all; then, as the tree gets older, stronger, and less bendable, the *teza* starts to develop as a tiny core surrounded by a very extensive 'white of egg'. Gradually, over many years, this proportion will change, so that in very old, very tall trees the *teza* will occupy most of the trunk, leaving a small outer ring of 'white of egg'. Such trees are the greatest and the most useful of all trees, since their *teza* can be used for the building of long-lasting houses and other artefacts which partake of the lasting nature of *teza* because they are made of it.

The presence of *teza* is awe-inspiring; it is a thing worthy of respect. It is the product of a maturation similar to the maturation of human beings in that it implies a straightening and a hardening of an inner core, but the *teza* of trees goes farther in that process than human beings can. Humans soon reach their peak of straightness and hardness and then go into reverse in old age and death; trees with *teza*, in contrast, continue to harden and become more and more lasting. As hard, dried wood, they outlast transitory human beings.

It is this lasting apotheosis of the *teza* of the noblest wood that is celebrated in the Zafimaniry carvings which are famous throughout Madagascar. These are low-relief geometrical patterns which cover the wooden parts of houses. Many writers have attempted with little success to understand what these carvings represent. In fact they represent nothing; they are a celebration of the lasting qualities of the *teza* which they cover.

WHAT HOUSES ARE LIKE

As is the case for people, marriages, and trees, the best way of understanding the Zafimaniry mental model of the house is to see it as a process of maturation. Indeed, the model of the maturation of the house is intimately tied to the model of the maturation of a marriage.

The first sign of appearance of a Zafimaniry house is usually the beginning of a flimsy building to the south of a young man's parents' house. Since a son owes his parents respect, this position is chosen because the south is an inferior direction to the north. The building will be very flimsy; apart from the four corner posts, it will be made of flexible woven bamboo and mats. It will most probably not possess the two focal features of the Zafimaniry house – the central house post, made of the *teza* of the hardest wood known to the Zafimaniry, and the hearth. These two crucial features are added only when the young man feels that his marriage is sufficiently well advanced to move his wife and children into the house. Then, with the permission of his father, he will erect the central house post and build the hearth. These will become the twin foci of the house. The central house post will be associated with the man for the rest of his life, and his normal place will be leaning against it. The hearth is little more than three stones which support a cooking pot and under which a fire can be lit. However, it will be furnished with the pots and cooking utensils which the bride brings with her after the *fanambarana* ceremony, and after that it will become permanently associated with the woman of the marriage. Before the house can be fully lived in, that is, before eating, cooking, or having sexual intercourse in it is allowed, a ritual of inauguration will be held wherein the elders of the families of both spouses will bless the house, especially the hearth and the central house post.

This ceremonial opening is, however, only a stage in a very long process during which the house will become harder and more permanent. What this means is that the soft and perishable parts of the house will gradually be replaced by the massive *teza* of great trees shaped so as to slot into each other. These are called the 'bones of the house', and they make the house extraordinarily lasting. The process of strengthening and beautifying the house is very long drawn out. It takes a long time for the house to become completely wooden, and before this some wood may already have had to be replaced. As the house is becoming more wooden, the wood itself will be gradually carved to 'celebrate' (to give *vonahitra* to) the *teza* of the posts, of the planks, and of the whole house itself. This hardening and beautifying is carried out at first by the husband working in marital cooperation with his 'male spouses', especially his wife's brothers. Then, as the spouses grow older, the task will be taken over by sons and daughters' husbands, then by grandsons and granddaughters' husbands, and so on. Thus the house which began with the marriage of two people will grow and become beautiful together with the fruitful balanced compatibility which they achieve. If the marriage continues to be fruitful, that is, if further descendants are born to it, this process of house growth will continue long after their death.

This is possible partly because of the unity of the group descended from a marriage and partly because of a symbolic substitution made conceivable by the association of people and trees via the notion of *teza*.[6] After the death of the couple the man will come to be represented by the central house post and the woman by the hearth and especially the furniture for it which she brought at her marriage. These remaining (*mateza*) objects become relics representing the original couple, and they are addressed as such and offerings are made to them by the descendants, especially on the occasions when they gather in the house, by then referred to as *trano masina* ('holy house'). These meetings will principally be to make requests for blessings from the house/ancestors and to settle disputes among descendants. A successful marriage therefore becomes an ever harder and more beautiful house which never stops growing as descendants in both male and female lines continue to increase. For these people it remains their 'house', though what this means is that it is a place of cult for them.

There is, however, a further aspect to all this. The couple in the house will itself have been the balanced product of two different houses: that of the parents of the bride and that of the parents of the groom. This fact is well recognized by the Zafimaniry. Thus young spouses with children, normally living in a house which has only just begun to harden with bones, are also children of two other couples. In fact, both the woman and the man are children of two couples, because, as we have seen, the marriage has made them the children of each other's parents. This dual filiation is demonstrated by the fact that the young couple and their children spend much time in the houses of their two sets of parents and will go and seek blessings from both sets whenever an important decision has to be made. In fact, of course, they will in theory also do this in the four sets of grandparents' houses, and so on, except that for these more remote ascendants it will not be the actual couples who are visited and asked for blessings but the paired house posts and hearths of holy houses.

It might seem as if everybody would belong to a near-infinity of ascendant houses, but the reality is usually much simpler. The reason is that the strong preference for marriages which overcome the imbalance caused by differences in gender (such as marriages between two pairs of cross-sex siblings) means that most marriages tend to occur between pairs of localities or moieties originating from two holy houses. The repetition of marriages means that most couples need only be concerned with two holy houses in which their respective groups originated as well as the two houses where their parents live. Intermediary houses tend to be forgotten.

THE CONCEPTUALIZATION OF SOCIETY

We have looked at five mental models of the sort which, according to connectionist theory, we would expect to be at the basis of people's conceptualizations of society. From my experience of life with the Zafimaniry these seem to me the central notions which organize these matters for them. To the Zafimaniry, and perhaps to us, these seem very 'obvious', very 'well-founded' observations of how things are. Yet we have seen how, when they are put together, they produce a distinctive conceptualization of society. Had we not proceeded in the way we did here – starting from these apparently 'obvious' understandings of 'how things are' – we would have ended with a description of Zafimaniry society which would have fallen foul of all the problems of misrepresentation I described in the introduction to this paper. This description would probably have been very similar to the account I gave in my first article on the Zafimaniry (Bloch 1975), and the reader who is in any doubt about the difference in the way ethnography is handled here from classical models should refer to that earlier attempt. The structure of the argument would be very familiar, and therefore acceptable, to other anthropologists, but it would suffer from the same problems of representing Zafimaniry ideas of society as if they took a logic-sentential form which in fact they do not take. Most probably, such an account would be totally foreign to the

Zafimaniry, whereas I am encouraged by the fact that they find the account presented here to be not 'alien' but so obvious that they think it pointless.

What, then, are the implications of going about things in this way? First, this account is much more likely to be compatible with theories which describe the mental/neural processes of storage and retrieval that people use in everyday life than would be the case for an account based on logic-sentential models. The Zafimaniry 'know' perfectly well that this is how people are and how they mature; they 'know' that trees grow like this and develop *teza*; it is 'obvious' that men and women are physiologically different, but it is equally 'obvious' that girls and boys are equally the children of their parents; 'clearly' a strong, hard, decorated house is the house of a couple whose children and other descendants are many and successful; it 'goes without saying' that a good marriage involves balance, cooperation, and mutuality. Of course, all this obviousness is ultimately misleading; anthropologists know, usually because they originate from another culture, what the informant does not know – that the 'obvious facts' are, partially at least, the product of specific and in the short term arbitrary historical processes. This, however, is not a reason for giving a false account of how people conceptualize their society.

In fact, there are other advantages in such an approach which can only be suggested here. The anchoring of conceptualization in the material – the body, houses, wood, styles of speaking – and in practices – cooking, cultivating, eating together – means that the cultural process cannot be separated from the wider processes of ecological, biological, and geographical transformation of which human society is a small part (a point made powerfully by Descola in this volume). Culture is not merely an interpretation superimposed on these material facts but integrated with them. When we are talking of mental processes, as we must when we are talking of conceptualization, we are talking of the interaction of one biological process with other biological and physical processes. Finally, seeing the conceptualization of society as flowing from mental models which are in great part conceptualizations of material things and practices suggests something about the way living in a society is learnt. It is not principally learnt by absorbing verbal rules and lexicographic definitions; rather it is learnt as one learns as a baby to negotiate the material aspect of one's house, as one follows other children in looking for berries in the forest, as one watches the stiff gait of one's grandfather, as one enjoys the pleasure of working harmoniously with a spouse, as one cooks with the implements of the hearth, as one sees one's grandfather lean against the central post, as one cuts through a massive tree trunk, and as one sees the beauty of the house of a fruitful marriage.[7]

NOTES

1 I carried out two prolonged periods of fieldwork among the Zafimaniry, for six months in 1971 and then for another six months in 1988–9. I was familiar with their culture and language before I started, having previously carried out fieldwork for several years among the closely related Merina. Previous accounts of the Zafimaniry include Vérin (1964), Coulaud (1973), Bloch (1975), and Raminosoa (1971–2). The research on which this paper is based was funded by a generous grant from the Spencer Foundation of Chicago. I am grateful for comments on earlier seminar presentations from members of the anthropology departments of the University of Bergen and the London School of Economics. Above all I am grateful for suggestions and help in preparing the manuscript from Fenella Cannell and J. Parry.

2 The term 'mental model' is Johnson-Laird's (1983). What I am referring to is similar to the 'cultural model' used by some anthropologists, but this term usually implies a reliance on language which I am trying to avoid (Holland and Quinn 1987).

3 The fact that these models are anchored in practice and material experience means that even to a non-Zafimaniry they may appear 'obvious'. This is significant, since such an approach rules out many of the wider claims of certain forms of cultural relativism.

4 I am ignoring variation within Zafimaniry culture in this account because when dealing with the fundamental models with which I am concerned I do not believe that there is much variation. This occurs at more superficial levels.

5 It is very interesting to compare this with the account of American marriage given by Quinn (1987). In many ways Quinn is aiming for the same kind of data as I am, but in contrast she depends almost exclusively on linguistic information.

6 This jump from people to things involves cognitive processes very different to those which can be discussed here (see Bloch 1991).

7 The parallel with Bourdieu's (1973) discussion of the Berber house will be clear, but differences arise from a completely different view of the nature of mental processes; Bourdieu uses precisely the logic-sentential notion of thought which I am criticizing here.

REFERENCES

Bechtel, W. (1990) 'Connectionism and the philosophy of mind: an overview', in W. Lycan (ed.) *Mind and Cognition*, Oxford: Blackwell.

Bloch, M. (1975) 'Property and the end of affinity', in M. Bloch (ed.) *Marxist Analyses and Social Anthropology*, London: Malaby Press.
——(1991) 'Language, anthropology, and cognitive science', *Man*. In press.
Bourdieu, P. (1972) *Esquisse d'une théorie de la pratique précédé de trois études d'ethnologie Kabyle*, Paris: Droz.
——(1973) 'The Berber house', in M. Douglas (ed.) *Rules and Meanings*, Harmondsworth: Penguin.
Churchland, P.S. and Sejnowski, T. (1989) 'Neural representation and neural computation', in L. Nadel, P. Cooper, P. Culicover, and R. Harnish (eds) *Neural Connections, Mental Computations*, Cambridge, MA: M.I.T. Press.
Coulaud, D. (1973) *Les Zafimaniry: Un groupe ethnique de Madagascar à la poursuite de la fôret*. Antanarivo: F.B.M.
Holland, D. and Quinn, N. (1987) *Cultural Models in Language and Thought*, Cambridge: Cambridge University Press.
Johnson-Laird, P. (1983) *Mental Models: Towards a Cognitive Science of Language, Inference, and Consciousness*, Cambridge: Cambridge University Press.
Quinn, N. (1987) 'Convergent evidence for a cultural model of American marriage', in D. Holland and N. Quinn (eds) *Cultural Models in Language and Thought*, Cambridge: Cambridge University Press.
Raminosoa, N. (1971–2) 'Système éducatif de la femme et sa fonction dans la société Zafimaniry', *Bulletin de Madagascar* 307: 936–51; 308: 3–30; 309: 107–39; 310: 215–34.
Reisman, K. (1974) 'Contrapuntal conversations in an Antiguan village', in R. Bauman and J. Sherzer (eds) *Explorations in the Ethnography of Speaking*, Cambridge: Cambridge University Press.
Vérin, P. (1964) 'Les Zafimaniry et leur art: un groupe continuateur d'une tradition esthètique Malgache méconnue', *Revue de Madagascar* 27: 1–76.

Name index

Subject index